Hope in the Wilderness

By

Brenda J Hester

He turns a wilderness into a pool of water

And a dry land into springs of water

Psalm 107:35

Copyright

To my husband Gary. Looking back at our life together, I am so amazed at how far the two of us have come. I am so thankful for you and your love for me. With the ups and downs, you encourage me to draw closer to God and to hear His voice for myself and what He was speaking to Me. You give me perspectives that are truly amazing through your own study of the word and your walk with God. You encourage me to dig deeper and find a true relationship with Jesus where I am able to hear His voice for myself. Thank you for all that you have sacrificed for me, the girls, and our grandchildren. All the hard word has not gone unnoticed. I Love You.

To my daughters Michelle and Rebecca. You have brought so much joy, frustration and love into my life. You gave me many times where trust and faith in Jesus was a must, and as I watch you now being mothers of your own children, I pray your children give you as much joy as the two of you have brought to my life. I love you both so very much.

To my friends that encouraged me to make this book, you have blessed me beyond measure. God has given me such a gift to have such Godly women in my life. Thank you for your friendship and encouragement. The laughter, (and with Kim there is always plenty of laughter), the coffee, (Brandi you make the best good strong coffee), and conversations. You have both inspired me in my pursuit of God and I thank you for everything. I love you my sisters in Christ.

To Pastor Mike and Kym., thank you for being there when we needed someone to guide us. Thank you for encouraging me to get out of my comfort zone especially in greeting and speaking to people. (Scary stuff). You guys have meant so much to me and Gary. I cannot express our love for you. Thank you for inspiring me to follow after the voice of God.

Day 1

"Let not your heart be troubled; you believe in God, believe also in Me."

John 14:1

A coincidence

Sometimes, quite often actually, we find that the things we are going through, praying for, and studying in scripture, all seem to line up with what we are hearing from the pulpit. God has a way of showing you what His word says, and confirming it again, and again. We think it's a coincidence, or maybe even, "isn't that funny"! We as Christians know there are no coincidences. God is speaking to us. "I hear you child. I know what you are going through. Let ME show you what the word says. See, here are some people that have gone through what you are going through, and I brought them through to the other side." The Word is alive, and goes out to preform what is was sent for. It is always showing itself to us, we must make ourselves open to hear from Him through it.

When all these things align themselves, it just means that He is with you. You and God form a majority, and you can ask whatsoever you desire, according to the word, with faith believing that you have what you asked for when you prayed, a nd it will be done. Know this; God knows your thoughts, knows your needs, knows your rising, and your setting. When all these things, align, Ask, Seek, and Knock. For whosoever asks, receives, whosoever seeks, finds, and whosoever knocks, the door will be opened to you.

Day 1

"For as the heavens are higher than the Earth, so are My ways higher than your ways, and My thoughts higher than your thoughts."

Isaiah 55:9

What things are happening in your life today, that makes you see God's hand in your situations and circumstances?

_____

_____

_____

_____

_____

_____

_____

_____

_____

_____

_____

_____

_____

_____

_____

_____

_____

_____

Day 2

"But He was wounded for our transgressions, He was bruised for our iniquities;
The chastisement was upon Him, and by His stripes we are healed."

Isaiah 53:5

Absolute trust in the spoken word of God.

The certain nobleman who came to Jesus for the healing of his servant, put absolute trust in Jesus. (Matthew 8:5-13). He knew that Jesus could heal him. The nobleman didn't keep urging Jesus to come home with him after He had spoken that the child was healed; he took Jesus at His word, and turned to go home; only to be met by a servant who told him that the servant was healed. He realized, upon inquiry, that the time of the child's healing was the exact time that Jesus spoke.

I have a granddaughter that was born without the left side of her brain developed. Surgery to detach the left side of her brain was performed to help her have any normalcy she might have in life. We trusted God at His word that Jesus took stripes upon His back that she is healed.

When things don't seem to go the way that you intend them to go, you trust. When the doctors told us there was a 75% chance of my granddaughter not surviving the operation. we trusted. She came through perfectly. When the doctors told us that it would probably be five to seven days before she woke up from the surgery; we trusted. She was waking up as she came to the room from surgery. When the doctors said she would probably never use the right side of her body; we trusted. She walks, and runs, and in 2019, she participated in her first year of cheerleading. When the doctors told us she is blind in her right eye; we trusted, and God made a creative, medically verifiable miracle. She not only sees in her right eye, but she never even developed the part of the brain that makes her see. She has almost 20-20 vision.

"Trust in the Lord, and lean not to thine own understanding, acknowledge Him

and He will direct your paths."

Proverbs 3:5&6

God's word is the authority over every situation, and circumstance you face today. The word says that life and death are in the power of the tongue. Speak words of life. Trust the word of God. The Bible says in John 1: 1-2, "The Word was in the beginning with God, and the Word was God." John 1:14 says, "the Word became flesh and dwelt among us." Jesus is the Word, and when we speak the Word, we speak Jesus into that situation. So my friend, have absolute trust in the Word of God, and when you do, stand still and see the glory of God come shining through.

So what areas are you putting absolute trust in God for?

_____

_____

_____

_____

_____

_____

_____

_____

_____

_____

_____

_____

_____

_____

_____

_____

_____

_____

_____

"Knowing that the testing of your faith produces patience. But let patience have it's perfect work, that you may be perfect and complete, lacking nothing."

James 1:3

Trust in times of loneliness

In times of our lives when we are needing to hear from God, our level of patience, and faith are tested. "Do you hear me God? Are you even there?" In these times, frustration may try to seep in. A feeling of loneliness may try to take control of your thoughts. God's word says in Deuteronomy 31:8, "The Lord Himself goes before you; He will never leave you, nor forsake you. Do not be afraid; do not be discouraged." You can always be assured that God is with you, and He hears you when you pray. Many in the bible thought they were all alone going through a time of testing, like Job. (Job 1) Job lost everything, his house, children, even his health deteriorated. He thought he was alone in what he was suffering. No one understood what he was going through, or how he was feeling. Paul must have felt alone when he asked God repeatedly to take the thorn from him. God's response was, "My grace is sufficient." (2 Corn 12:9) What about the ultimate aloneness; Jesus on the cross. Even He cried out, "My God, My God, why have you forsaken me?" (Matthew 27:46)

There are times when we will all go through a feeling of being alone. Many times we feel alone even in a crowd. That's when we must be patient because God is working behind the scenes for your good. Standing still isn't always the easiest thing to do, but sometimes it's the best thing we can do. Moses said to the people, (see Exodus 14:13) "Stand still, and see the glory of God." as God parted the Red Sea for the Israelites to cross on DRY ground. If we try to rush ahead of God thinking we can do things ourselves; trying to work out a situation on our own, it may ultimately lead to more frustration, and a deeper feeling of loneliness. "Let Me" says God. "I will go before you, and fight your battles. I will make your crooked paths straight. I will mount you up on wings as eagles, and make you soar. I will; because I AM. Trust Me. I AM working all things for your good."

"Strengthened with all might, according to His glorious power, for all patience and longsuffering with joy,"

What areas in your life is God working on you to develop patience?

_____

_____

_____

_____

_____

_____

_____

_____

_____

_____

_____

_____

_____

_____

_____

_____

_____

"Day 4

"And my God shall supply all your need according to His riches and glory in Christ

Jesus"

Philippians 4" 19

What fragments do you carry?

After the feeding of the five thousand, the disciples took up twelve baskets of bread fragments. Seeing what Jesus had done, they carried the fragments with them, as a reminder of the miracle that Jesus performed. (See Matthew 14: 13-21)

After being saved, and accepting Jesus as Lord of your life, people still carry fragments of their past with them. However, soon they see that it is the Word, or the Bread of Life that sustains them as they go. The Bread, or Word, is a form of communion. A remembrance of what God has done. It isn't about the food, it's about the miracle. Your life is changed at the moment that you accept Jesus as Lord, and Savior. You have become a new creation. God has changed your whole makeup, and washed all your sins in the sea of forgetfulness to be remembered no more.

But what about the fragments? I still have stuff that I am carrying. The hurt and consequences of my past are still there. Trust the Word of God. When you do, He will bring about a change in you, that will then, bring about the change around you. It's as if God is saying to us, at that time, "I will provide all that you need to overcome. I Am enough, and more. Don't look at the natural seas that are raging, look at the miracle that was done. You're name is written in the Lambs Book of Life. You will have an everlasting life with Jesus in heaven. Soon the basket of fragments will get more empty as you walk with, and trust in the working power of the Holy Spirit inside of you. I know your needs, and I will supply your needs according to My riches in glory. Trust Me. I am working all things for your good."

God will ultimately make every situation, no matter how bad it may be, for your good. You may not see it now, but looking back, you will see that it had to happen the way it did, for the outcome that it had. Keep your eyes on Jesus, trusting in His Word to perform what it says it will do. Soon the fragments of your past will take on a different form, and fall away, as you trust in the miracle of the saving grace of Christ Jesus.

"Day 4

"And gave them bread from heaven for their hunger, and brought them water out of the rock for their thirst, and told them to go in to possess the land which You had sworn to give them."

Nehemiah 9:15

What fragments are you carrying from your past that you are trusting God to do a miracle work?

_____

_____

_____

_____

_____

_____

_____

_____

_____

_____

_____

_____

_____

_____

_____

"Ask of the Lord rain in the time of the latter rain. The Lord will make flashing clouds: He will give them showers of rain, grass in the field for everyone."

Zechariah 10: 1

Desert Worship

Are you feeling like you are going through the dry seasons of life? Are you feeling parched as if in a desert? Do your prayers feel like they are hitting a wall? What you need, is a good refreshing rain. God said ," I will give you rain in due season, and the land shall yield her increase, and the trees of the field yield their fruit." (Leviticus 26:4) We all go through seasons in our lives. The word says, "For everything there is a season, a time for every activity under heaven." (Eccl 3:1) In this time of dry parched seasons, take time to inventory. "Am I doing all I can for God? Am I studying, and meditating on the word? Am I keeping myself in position to hear the voice of the Holy Spirit?" Look at yourself, and ask the Holy Spirit to shine His light on you. Ask Him to reveal to you if you are where you are supposed to be. Then lift yourself up in in your most holy faith as David did in worship, and reminding yourself of Whose you are.

Things weren't always going the way King David intended them to go, but David knew how to pick himself up, and give praise to God for all things. (see Psalm 34) In the times of drought, remember the things that God has done for you. Look back and see how far God has brought you. We aren't always where we want to be, but praise Jesus we aren't where we used to be. Let even the smallest of things that He has done for you, bless you, and let the remembrance start to stir those rain clouds. God is a refreshing God. Get alone with Him, and worship Him. God inhabits the praises of His people. When you worship and remind yourself of how much God loves you, the rain clouds will start to appear on the horizon, and it will lift up your spirit, to yield the increase, and bring forth fruit. Soaking your dry parched souls, making them come alive. "Ask of the Lord rain in the time of the latter rain. It is the Lord who makes lightnings which usher in the rain and gives men showers and grass in the field." (Zech 10:1)

Rain on us Holy Spirit, refresh our souls. Make us to lie down in green pastures and lead us beside still waters. (Psalm 23)

Day 5

"Then He will give the rain for your seed, with which you sow the ground, and bread of the increase of the earth, and it will be fat and plentiful."

Isaiah 30:23

Write down your best worship and praise to God, to be a reminder to look back at and remember.

_____

_____

_____

_____

_____

_____

_____

_____

_____

_____

_____

_____

_____

_____

_____

_____

_____

_____

"Day 6

Jesus said to her, "Did I not say to you that if you would believe you would see the
glory of God?"
John 11:40

Supernaturally Possible

"Lazarus come out!" and out walked the man who had been dead for three days. His hands, and feet wrapped in burial cloths, and a napkin around his face. Jesus said to them, "Free him of the burial wrappings and let him go" The voice of authority calling out to the dead. "Arise", and from the dead he came. (See John 11:1-44)

Jesus gave the people a demonstration of what would soon happen to Himself in the resurrection. He would soon show that death has no power over Him. "Free him from the burial wrappings" was a foretaste of what was about to happen to Himself, and ultimately to all those who die in Christ. Jesus told Martha, "Did I not tell you, and promise you, that if you would believe and rely on Me, you would see the glory of God?" We are all to rely explicitly on the Word of God to perform what He would have it to. Jesus prayed to heaven so the people could hear Him say to God, " I know You always hear, and listen to Me." Jesus spoke to God, in their presence, so they would understand the authority that was His to perform the miracle He was about to do. Jesus spoke, "Lazarus come forth," and the impossible became supernaturally possible.

With God, all things are possible to them that believe. Jesus said " I assure you, most solemnly I tell you, if anyone steadfastly believes in Me, he will himself be able to do the things I do; and he will do even greater things than these, because I go to the Father, and I will ask the Father, and He will send you a comforter that He may remain with you forever." The Holy Spirit is sent to all believers at the time of salvation, through the death, burial, and resurrection of Jesus, and our belief in Him. Through that belief, we have been given the authority over death, hell and the grave. It no longer has dominion over you. The world was spoke into being. Just as Jesus spoke to the grave and out walked Lazarus.

Day 6

"Jesus said unto her, "I am the resurrection and the life, he that believes in Me, though he may die, yet shall he live."

John 11:25

Speak to your situations today, and with faith believing that when you pray, you receive what you ask the moment that you pray, you will see your answers come walking up out of the grave, and always remember, God hears you when you pray.

Write out your prayer to God today. What are you believing for? Remember, when you pray He hears you?

_____

_____

_____

_____

_____

_____

_____

_____

_____

_____

_____

_____

_____

_____

_____

_____

_____

"Hear me when I call, O God of my righteousness! You have relieved me in my distress; have mercy upon me and hear my prayer."

Psalms 4: 1

God's Own Image

"What's that in your hand?" God asked Moses. "It's only a rod."

When God asks you a question, there is a very good reason for that question. "Oh this? It's just my rod. It's just my story. It's no big deal." God says, "I can use that." When you open yourself up to hear from God, then you open yourself up to the possibility of being used in a manner you thought never would come to you. "Me? You want me? I don't have an education. I don't know how to talk to people." Moses said " I am slow of speech, and have a heavy tongue." (See Exodus 4:10-12)

Why are we so quick to put ourselves down at the thought of God using us in a mighty way. God not only created us, but He created us in His image. We were made for this. We were made to be supernatural beings set apart, different, and peculiar. He made us to be His hands, His feet, and His mouth. Jesus commissioned the apostles to go forth, and preach the word to all the world. They were given an assignment so much greater than they: a fisherman, a tax collector. What are you? A teacher, a logger, a stay at home mom. Whatever you identify yourself as, God sees you as a worker for His kingdom.

What do you have in your hand? You have the keys that set people free from destruction. In your hand is life, because you hold the thoughts feelings, and purposes of Christ heart in you. When you walk in habitual lockstep with God, He goes before you to make your paths great. He orders your footsteps, and makes your feet like hind's feet that run, and not grow warry. You have everything you need for this day right inside of you. Just as God called Moses, and asked " What's in your hand?" God is asking you. " What's in your hand? I can use that. Will you use it for My glory, and be My mouthpiece, My hands, My own peculiar people?

Will You?"

"God be merciful to us and bless us: and cause His face to shine upon us."

Psalms 67:1

What do you feel like the Lord has laid on your heart to do for the kingdom?

_____

_____

_____

_____

_____

_____

_____

_____

_____

_____

_____

_____

_____

_____

_____

_____

_____

_____

_____

_____

_____

"For He will deliver you from the snare of the fowler and from the deadly pestilence…
You shall not be afraid of the terror of the night, nor of the arrow that flies by day."

Psalms 91:3

Let it Go

"Unless these men remain in the ship, you cannot be saved. Then the soldiers cut away the ropes that held the small boat, and watched it fall and drift away."
(See Acts 27)

What's your boat? What is in your life that you need to cut, and let drift away because it's keeping your life in turmoil? The waves keep crashing around, the wind is howling, but you keep trying to escape in the small boat. Let it go. It's not the best for you. Whatever hinders your walk with God must be taken out of your life. Is it your past? Is it unforgiveness? Bitterness? Do you maybe need to forgive yourself? Maybe it's not that at all, but something in your life that you are doing. Drugs, alcohol, pornography, maybe even over eating. Whatever it is that is causing you to be in turmoil, God says, "Let it go. Let it drop from the boat and drift away."

Jesus came to Paul in the night, and said, "I am with you," just as He comes to all of us in our midnight hours when we cry out to Him for help. But for Paul, He did have a prerequisite, "You must stay on the boat, and you will be saved." Jesus my friend is our boat of refuge. If we stay with Him, even though there are nor-easters in our life, we will be saved. He is always there to calm the seas. Just as He did for the disciples when they were crossing the sea to the other side. The wind and waves began to blow in such ferocity they were in fear of their lives. They rushed to wake up Jesus who was sleeping so peacefully. "Don't you care if we parish?" They shouted to Jesus. He wasn't concerned, He was sleeping. "Peace be still", was all He had to say, and the wind, and waves obeyed. He then turned to the disciples and said, "Oh ye of little faith." He was teaching them, that they, as we do today, have the power to calm the seas.

"The Lord is your keeper: the Lord is your shade at your right hand.

Psalms 121:5

Don't let the waves of your life keep you in perpetual seasickness. Speak to them. Know that when you speak to the Father, He hears you; and if you speak with faith believing, the wind and the waves must obey. For the greater One lives in you. "Unless these men remain on the ship, you cannot be saved." He said. Stay on the ship that is Jesus . Wrap the ropes of God's word around you, and speak to the waves. Open your eyes to see the clouds part, and the sun shine with a glorious new day, knowing that His mercies are new every morning.

"What do you fear most that you can trust God to help you overcome?

_____

_____

_____

_____

_____

_____

_____

_____

_____

_____

_____

_____

_____

_____

_____

_____

_____

_____

"Lean on, trust in, and be confident in the Lord with all your heart and mind and do not rely on your own insight or understanding"

Proverb 3:5

Be ye separate

As the plagues were being brought upon the Egyptians, God was revealing to them, and the world, that the Israelites were His people. "That you may know the Lord makes a distinction between the Egyptians, and Israelites." None of the plagues affected them in any way. As darkness fell over Egypt, the land of Goshen was bathed in light. (Exodus 7:14-12:40)

Today, we believers, are to be light in this dark, and dying world. We are to go forth, and spread that light, by sharing the good news to those who do not know, or believe. God has called us to "come out, and be ye separate." He makes that distinction. We are in this world, but we as believers are called not be of this world. The Word of God is the light that shines out from every believer, to help others see that the only thing they need in this world is a relationship with Jesus. "Believe on Me. Trust in My word, and I will show you great, and mighty things that you know not." God is saying this to every believer, and non-believer.

When a doctor's report comes that is scary, the darkness can be engulfing. We know that Jesus is our healer. He took stripes upon His back that we be healed. When you lose your job, and don't know how you're going to get the necessities you, and your family need; the days can be hard to get through. But God says "He will provide all your needs according to His riches in glory through Christ Jesus to them that believe." (Phil 4:19) The Word says, "For I know the thoughts and plans that I have for you," says the Lord, " plans for welfare and peace, and not for evil, to give you hope in your final outcome." (Jeremiah 29:11) God does all things for good to those who believe on Him, lean on Him, trust on Him. When the enemy comes, you have an advocate in Jesus. He is ever interceding for you before the throne of God. He loves you with an everlasting love. Psalms 54 says, "God is my helper, and ally' the Lord is my upholder...for He has delivered me out of every trouble." He wants to be your helper, and deliverer. He wants you to lay your burdens down at His feet. He says in Matthew 11:28, "Come unto Me, all ye that labor and are heavy laden and I will give you rest."

"Commit your way to the Lord; trust also in Him; and He shall bring it to pass."
Psalms 37:5

Just as God brought the Israelites out of Egypt, guiding them with a cloud by day, and a pillar of fire by night, He too will bring you out of your Egypt. He will guide you by His word, and the voice of the Holy Spirit. Let Jesus be that pillar of fire in your darkest days, being the light of Goshen, where He makes the distinction of those who believe, and trust in Him.

My friends, what is your Egypt? Where is God bringing you from? What is God shining His light on, to show you the distinction that you are His chosen child?

_____

_____

_____

_____

_____

_____

_____

_____

_____

_____

_____

_____

_____

_____

_____

_____

_____

_____

_____

_____

"For I know the thoughts that I think towards you, says the Lord, thoughts of peace and not of evil, to give you a future and a hope."

Jeremiah 29:11

True Freedom

Where does true freedom come from? Man would have you to believe that true freedom come from doing whatever makes you happy. Unfortunately, we as humans really don't know what makes us happy. We think things like, "That promotion will make me happy." Will it? The extra hours at the office, the extra stress. Is that true freedom? Freedom isn't more, it's less. The more you have, the more you have to do to keep that more. Freedom isn't a place, what we do, or how we live. True freedom comes through a relationship with Jesus Christ. Jesus said, "If you abide in My word, you are truly My disciples, and you will know the Truth, and the Truth will set you free."

What is the Truth? The Truth is Jesus. He sets you free from the bondages that hinder you. People say that you have the freedom to worship as you wish. Do you really? The Truth says, "Those that climb up any other way is as a thief and a liar. (See John 10:1) "Unless you be born again, you cannot enter the kingdom of heaven." (See John 3:3) Man would say that you have the freedom to choose even what sex you marry. Really? Do you? The Truth says, "For this reason, a man shall leave his father and mother and shall be united to his wife, and the two shall become one flesh." (See Matthew 19:5)

In the days of Judges, the word says," They all did what was right in their own eyes. (Judges 21:25) It didn't fare well for the Israelites of the time. When people do what's right in their own eyes, Satan will use that, to make their flesh desire what is not natural. They followed after other gods, and set up idols in their homes. It was an abomination to God. War was always in their midst because of their rebellion from the commandments of God.

We must keep our eyes on Jesus, to reach the pinnacle of freedom that He has in store for all of those who believe in Him. When you ask the Holy Spirit to reveal to you the deepest things in your heart and mind that must be dealt with, to experience total freedom, He will. It is possible to rid yourself of fleshly desires, and replace them with the desires of Christ.

The council of the Lord stands for ever, the plans of His heart to all generations.
Psalms 33:11

Just as Jesus said to God in the garden awaiting the cross, "Not my will, but Your will be done," we too must surrender ourselves to the Savior, and let Him do the work in us to bring us the freedom that only He can bring. A freedom to not have to sin. A freedom of peace and security, knowing you have a heavenly home awaiting you.

What do you think God is wanting to set you free from today?

_____

_____

_____

_____

_____

_____

_____

_____

_____

_____

_____

_____

_____

_____

_____

_____

_____

"If you confess with your mouth, the Lord Jesus and believe in your heart that God has raised Him from the dead, you will be saved."

Romans 10:9-20

In Christ

In Christ. What does that really mean to be **in Christ**? Romans 10:9-10 says "If you confess with your lips that Jesus is Lord, and in your heart believe that God raised Him from the dead you will be saved,"

When we are drawn by the Holy Spirit to give up ourselves, and accept Jesus as our Lord and Savior, we become a new creation. Our old nature is dead, and a new nature **in Christ** takes hold. Many are taught that we invite Jesus into our lives, and hearts, and become Christians (born again). The Word would bear witness that it is we who are invited **in Christ**. Our lives are to be conformed to Jesus' nature. Jesus being the savior of man, came out of His deity to save the world through His shed blood sacrifice on the cross. When we are born again, we accept Christ (the anointed Godhead), into our hearts, and we are conformed to the image of Jesus (son of man, high priest, savior) who became flesh and dwelt among us. We become like Him. We become **in Christ** who is the creator of the world, the Word of God.

There is a distinction of Jesus Christ the anointed redeemer, and Christ Jesus, the Anointed Spirit Himself. The bible says that we are **in Christ** (Christ Jesus the Anointed spirit). We are the body of Christ (spirit) not the body of Jesus (flesh). Christ (spirit) lives in me, not Jesus (man). We are heirs, and joint heirs with Jesus (man). He's our heavenly brother. We put on Jesus' nature, so that our flesh, and soul can be conformed, but we accept **in** us, Christ Jesus the anointed spirit who helps us to conform to the image of Jesus.

It's the spirit Christ that raises up your mortal bodies through the spirit that dwells in us. Romans 8:11. The bible does not say we are in Jesus, but **in Christ.** So to sum, we are heirs with Jesus. We take on Jesus skin. We are conformed to Him, we accept into our hearts, Christ Jesus the anointed savior to be led by the Spirit of God.

Day 11

"But if the Spirit of Him who raised Jesus from the dead dwells in you, He who raised Christ from the dead will also give life to your mortal bodies through His Spirit who dwells in you."

Romans 8:11

Are you in Christ? Write your testimony of how you accepted Jesus as your savior for a reminder of what He has done for you.

_____

_____

_____

_____

_____

_____

_____

_____

_____

_____

_____

_____

_____

_____

_____

"And let us not grow weary while doing good, for in due season we shall reap if we do not lose heart."

Galatians 6:9

Stepping Out of Bondage

"Little by little I will drive them out from before you until you have increased, and are numerous enough to take possession of the land." God said, "Go in. Take possession. I have given you the land flowing with milk, and honey. (See Leviticus 20:24) I have delivered you from the hand of the Egyptians, and have given you my commands. You are a mighty nation. Now move and I will be with you. Joshua 1:9 says, "Be strong and of good courage; do not be afraid, nor be dismayed, for the Lord your God is with you wherever you go."

Coming out of Egypt was a hard thing to do, having been in bondage for so many years they forgot how to live a life of freedom. But that is exactly what He was giving them. God told the Israelites to go forward. They must have been in fear of the unknown. But God kept telling them to move and trust Him. "Then all the congregation of the children of Israel moved on from the Wilderness of Sin by stages." (Exodus 17:1)

Just as the Israelites were to trust God to move forward, we also must trust Him to move forward through the wilderness areas in our lives where we can't see the way through the trees. Proverb 3:5-6 says, "Trust in the Lord with all your heart, and do not lean to your own understanding. In all your ways acknowledge Him, and He will direct your paths."

I was a sickly child. In and out of hospitals a lot as a kid. I never developed the ability to converse well with people. I was alone quite a bit. As I grew to adulthood, I developed the bondage of shyness. I didn't know how to talk to people. It was hard at first when my pastor kept telling me to speak to people. "Go greet them, they are new." He would tell me. He pushed me, over and over until I started to freely walk up to people and greet them. Little by little the fear left me. I now am a greeter at our church helping to make new comers first experience a warm welcome. It just takes trust, and stepping out.

"Do not be afraid. Stand still, and see the salvation of the Lord. Which he will accomplish for you today."

Exodus 14:13

We must step out of our comfort zones, even when those comfort zones are bondages. When you do, you will see the hope for the future that He has planned for you. He is there to open up the way for you. He says "Thy word is a lamp unto my feet, and a light unto my path." He makes the paths straight. Trust the Word, and He will bring you from glory to glory, shining brighter, and brighter, to that glorious day.

Little by little God changes us, and situations and circumstances in our lives. What changes can you see in your life that were made, little by little?

_____
_____
_____
_____
_____
_____
_____
_____
_____
_____
_____
_____
_____
_____
_____
_____
_____
_____
_____

"Day 13
"That He may grant you a spirit of wisdom, and revelation of insight, into mysteries
, and secrets in the deep and intimate knowledge of Him."

Ephesians 1:17

Trust Me

"It's time," the nurses said as they came to get my granddaughter to wheel her into surgery. "It's going to be about an eight hour procedure. We will call you every hour to give you an update on how she is doing." There were so many people there as they wheeled my tiny, helpless, two-month old granddaughter through the surgical doors, headed for a brain surgery that would change the rest of her life. We, as well as many others were praying, and believing God for a miracle. We waited, trusting in Jehovah Rapha our healer.

Sometimes you are going through life, and it's good. "I am going to be a grandmother. A beautiful baby girl. Her name is going to be Chloe Ann. I can't wait to see her. Ann was my mother's middle name, who has already passed on." Excitement and anticipation of my grand-daughters coming. Then she does, and something isn't quite right. After going back and forth from the emergency room for days, you finally get a nurse to stop long enough to see what you see. They give you the news. "The left side of her brain isn't developed. It is causing her brain to seize constantly. If something isn't done shortly, it could potentially damage the right side beyond repair, and she may not have any kind of productive life." The news hits you like a bat to the stomach. How? You cry out to God, why? "My grace is sufficient," (2 Corn 12:9) is the only answer from God. James 1:6 says, "When you ask, you must not doubt". Yes, I do trust you Lord.

Jesus took stripes upon His back so that we are healed. People would say "God works in mysterious ways," But does He? No, really He doesn't not to those who believe. Ephesians 1:8-9 says, " He lavished upon us every kind of wisdom, and understanding. Making known to us the mystery of His will." His will is that we are healed. The Word is God, and if we study and show ourselves approved, rightly dividing the word of God, then we will know His character, and His will in situations, and circumstances. There is an answer for everything in the Word of God. Even when you don't seem to get an answer He says, "My grace is sufficient."

"O Lord my God, I cried out to you, and You healed me."
Psalms 30:2

What started out as devastating news, turned into a miracle. My granddaughter, is now eight, seizer free from the day of surgery, and although she has only the right side of her brain; she is healthy, walking, talking and seeing. You see, they never thought she would walk, but she does. They never thought she would see, but she does. "Trust Me. My grace is sufficient," Is all the answer we received from God.

When we trusted, a miracle walked through our door. So when faced with unsurmountable odds, look up from where your help comes from, and believe.

For His grace IS SUFFICIENT.

What miracles are you looking up for ?

_____

_____

_____

_____

_____

_____

_____

_____

_____

_____

_____

_____

_____

_____

_____

"Therefore do not sin reign in your mortal body, that you should obey it in it's lusts."

Romans 6:12

Victory over your enemies

"And it was told Joshua, saying, 'The five kings are found in a cave at Merkabah,' and Joshua said, 'Roll great stones upon the mouth of the cave, and set men by it for to keep them; and stay not, but pursue after the enemies, and smite the hindmost of them; for the Lord your God hath delivered them into your hand,'" (see Joshua 10:16-27)

Joshua was facing the armies of five kings. His faith was tested. It is often stated that to have great faith, you must be tested greatly. Joshua was at war. "Fear them not; for I have delivered them into thine hand; there shall not a man of them stand before thee." (Joshua 10:8) God wants us to face those things in our lives that keep us bound, keeping us from the best of what God has in store for us. Keeping us from our destinies. Joshua obeyed God, and because he did, God went before him to defeat the enemy. God never told him it was going to easy, God said "Fear not," It's as if God was saying, "I got this. They can't overcome you, because I AM all you need to defeat your enemies. Trust Me. I have a better life waiting for you on the other side of your battle."

Joshua had a great victory. Are there things in your life that you need to defeat? Is your flesh getting in the way of a deeper walk with God? We must put to death our fleshly desires, the things that keep us bound. What is it that you are dealing with? Smoking? Drinking? Is it your weight? Just because you aren't going out and fighting a physical enemy like Joshua, you are fighting a very real enemy within. The one that keeps you from obtaining the best that God has for you. We are the temple of God. We are to, as Paul said, "Buffet our bodies." (1Corn 9:27) We are to bring our bodies into subjection, to be the temple that God can use in the spiritual warfare that takes place in our lives. When God is telling you to crucify your flesh, He knows by going through it, you can experience a deeper, more fulfilling walk with Him. Jesus even struggled with His flesh when He was in the garden. "If this cup could pass from Me, but not My will, but Yours be done." (Matthew 26:39)

Day 14

"Watch and pray, that ye enter not into temptation: the spirit is willing but the flesh is weak:

Matthew 26:41

Like Joshua that bound the king's in the cave to pursue the enemy until they were completely killed off, we must also put our bodies in the cave of subjection, to pursue after our enemies that keep us in a bondage to our flesh. Overcoming the enemies of our flesh, the secret things that no one knows about, but God. It is then that we will experience the freedom, and blessings that God has in store for us from the beginning. So put on your armor, and go to war. The battle is waging, but we can do all things through Christ who strengthens us.

Write down some scriptures to meditate on that will help you to overcome the flesh.

"Blessed is the man that walketh not in the counsel of the ungodly, nor standeth in the way of sinners nor sits in the seat of the scornful. But his delight is in the law of the Lord; and in his law doth he meditate day and night."

Psalms 1:1-2

Rooted and Grounded in Jesus

Are you firmly rooted? Are you planted by the rivers of living water? (Psalm 1:1-3) Are your roots are deep in the water when all others around you are in a dry season? Are your roots finding that hidden water that only comes when you seek Jesus who IS the Living Water, with your whole heart?

God is asking us; are we that tree? Are you seeking God and His word as if you cannot go a single moment, or take a single breath without Him? "Seek Me, and you will find Me, when you search for ME, with your whole heart." (Jeremiah 29:13). "Call to Me, and I will show you great and mighty things that you know not." (Jeremiah 33:3) "He shall be like a tree planted by the rivers of water that brings forth its fruit in it's season, whose leaf shall not wither; and whatever he does shall prosper." (Psalm 1:3) The word says in Ephesians 1:4 that God chose you. "Just as He chose us in Him before the foundation of the world, that we would be holy and blameless before Him." Open yourself to God and let Him show you, all that He is. He is, I Am, and He is all you need. He is El Shaddai, the all sufficient one. Don't seek the attention of man, but keep your eyes on the One who saves, and let Him fill you with all that your heart desires. God loves you with an everlasting love. Let Him in every part of your life, for He is Jehovah Jireh (your provider) when you are in need. He is Jehovah Shalom (your peace) when the storms are raging. He is Jehovah Rafah (your healer) when the doctors report isn't good. He is the I AM that you need. For He is El Elyon (the God Most High) the One you can put your trust in."

Day 15

"But He answered and said, "Every plant, which my heavenly Father hath not planted, shall be rooted up."

Matthew 15:13

How are your roots firmly rooted? What are doing to make sure that you are grounded in good soil so you bear much fruit?

_____

_____

_____

_____

_____

_____

_____

_____

_____

_____

_____

_____

_____

_____

_____

_____

_____

_____

_____

_____

_____

_____

Day 16

"It is an old leprosy on the skin pf his body. The priest shall pronounce him unclean,
and shall not isolate him, for he is unclean."

Leviticus 13:11-13

What is your leprosy?

When man goes through a trial, or test, things can become very raw. Emotions are high, and you may be feeling like you are on a rollercoaster. One day you may be good, but watch out, there is a curve up ahead, and it's about to get steep. Your emotions are raw. You can't think, or act on the level of faith to overcome. You are reaching out to things, and solutions other than God. You become helpless to the attack. You my friend, may becoming unclean. For whatever does not originate, and proceed from faith is sin.

When something wasn't right on a person's body, a spot or blemish, in the days of Moses, (See Leviticus 13) the people would go and present themselves to the priest, and the priest would look at them, watch, and minister to them for a period of seven days to determine if they had leprosy. Today, Jesus is our high priest. When the test, and trials come, and you find yourself in a very raw situation, let Jesus minister, and watch over you. Go to Him like they did to the priests; show Jesus your raw places. Give him the hurt, the sickness, because Jesus is your healer. He took the stripes upon Himself for you to be healed. Present yourself, your situation, your hurt, your shame to Him, and let Him be Lord over all your leprosy. Trust Jesus to be all that you need. Psalm 23 says, "The Lord is my shepherd I shall not want. He makes me to lie down in green pastures; He leads me beside still waters. He restores my soul; He leads me in the paths of righteousness for His name's sake. Yea, though I walk through the valley of the shadow of death, I will fear no evil; for You are with me." Don't let another minute of your day go by without calling on the I Am. For He is all you need.

In the days of Moses, if the leprosy covered the whole body and turned white, the person was declared clean. When the cleansing blood of Jesus covers your leprosy, you are also white as snow. Isaiah 1:18 says, "Though your sins are like scarlet, they shall be as white as snow." You are clean from your sin. You are whole. You are all that He says you are. You are a child of the Most High God. Let Jesus wash you from whatever leprosy you carry, and let the rollercoaster come to the station so you can get off, and walk a life of freedom and be clean.

"Create in me a clean heart, O God; and renew a right spirit within me"
Psalms 51:10

What areas of your life are you needing to bring into the rollercoaster station so you can get off?

_____

_____

_____

_____

_____

_____

_____

_____

_____

_____

_____

_____

_____

_____

_____

"But He said, 'More than that, blessed are those who hear the word of God and keep it."

Luke 11:28

The Bread of Life

"They gathered manna every morning, each one as much as he needed, for when the sun became hot it melted." (See Exodus 16:21) Each morning brings a new day, a new set of circumstances that will have to be dealt with. The Israelites relied on the manna from heaven to feed them, or they would starve. They trusted that each morning the food would be there, but those who didn't get up early enough. didn't get any, because like the word said, "when the sun became hot it melted away." (Exodus 16:21) They were left without the nourishment they needed to go through the daily grind.

This is so like people today. God has given us His word which is the Bread of Life, to feast upon. He would have us to digest it each day, so when the sun gets hot, and the cares, and situations of our everyday lives start to encroach upon us, we will be full of what the word says. We will be able to apply that word, stand on that word, and make the food work for us. As we pour ourselves out through the day, "the word is a lamp to our feet and a light to our path." (Psalm 119:105) When you are in traffic, and it doesn't seem to be moving in a hurry, remember, "let patience have her perfect work, that you may be perfect, and not lacking anything." (Jame1:4-6) The word says that we will be able to bear up under anything, and everything that comes because we ate. We got full. We feasted on the Bread of Life. "It's health to your navel, and marrow to your bones." (Proverbs 3:8) Jesus said, "This is the bread that came down from heaven. It isn't like the manna which our forefathers ate, and yet died; he who takes this Bread for his food shall live forever. (John 6:58)

Gather up your manna in the early dawn of morning where God's mercies are new every day, and let it give you the strength to take on the world. For His word says, we have all authority over the world, the flesh, and the devil.

Day 17

"You also gave Your good Spirit to instruct them. And did not withhold Your manna from their mouth, and gave them water for their thirst"

Nehemiah 9:20

How has God provided the manna you needed to sustain you?

_____

_____

_____

_____

_____

_____

_____

_____

_____

_____

_____

_____

_____

_____

_____

_____

_____

_____

_____

_____

_____

_____

_____

"Day 18

"Immediately the Spirit drove Him into the wilderness"

Mark 1:12

Let God lead you

Paul was on his way back to Jerusalem. He was at one time the strictest of Pharisee. A persecutor of the Way. He was headed to go back and tell them of his conversion to Jesus Christ, as if he felt that he needed to share his story, and the gospel with the people. Maybe in the hope that they too would become followers of Jesus. Along the way, where he stopped, disciples "prompted by the Holy Spirit," kept telling Paul not to set foot in Jerusalem. Still he was determined to go.

(See Acts 21)

Agabus, a prophet, "prompted by the Holy Spirit", demonstrated to Paul with binds on his wrists, what would happen to him if he was to go to Jerusalem. But Paul went anyway. Upon reaching Jerusalem, Paul met with the disciples, and after purification, entered the temple to preach. He had good intentions. He went back to where his greatest sins were committed to convert the people. He went back even though along the way the Holy Spirit warned, "Don't go". There will be consequences to your decisions. Paul was met with anger by the people. God told him, "Hurry get quickly out of Jerusalem, because they will not receive your testimony about me." Paul pleaded, "but God, I cast into prison and flogged those who believed on You, and when the blood of Your witness Stephen was shed, I also was personally standing by and consenting and approving, and guarding the garments of those who slew him." Paul wanted so badly to fix what he had done. God said to him, "Go, I will send you far away unto the Gentiles." Was it possible that Paul started to go back out of God's will, to try to fix his own past mistakes? God knew what he was doing, and knew they wouldn't receive him. We can't go back and fix what was in our past. Sometimes you have to let it be. But God was with him because his heart was right?

Would Paul have gone through such persecution had he followed the prompting of the Holy Spirit and not gone to Jerusalem? We can never know, but we do know, God was with him. When we do things on our own, even if it's a great thing for God, but God didn't ordain for you to do it, there will be consequences for it. We must be obedient to the voice of the Holy Spirit. When we do, we will then have the grace to accomplish all that God has for us to do. The Holy Spirit warned Paul all along the journey. Was He preparing Paul's heart for what lie ahead? Will God bless you anyway? Yes, you see here that Paul did get to preach to many unbelievers, and we are able to follow his letters some 2000 plus years later. God was with him, because his heart was in the right place.

"Has the Lord as great delight in burnt offerings and sacrifices, as in obeying the voice of the Lord? Behold, to obey is better than sacrifice"

1 Samuel 15:22

Was it possible that with going his own way, and not waiting to hear what God had planned, there were consequences. Prison, beatings, and shipwrecks. Ask the Holy Spirit; seek His promptings. "Where do You want me to go? What do You want me to do? What is it You want me to say? Not my will, but Yours be done." When you do, blessings will overtake you and bring you into a broad place..

Ask the Holy Spirit what He would have you to do, and write what you hear. Then go and obey the voice of God.

_____

_____

_____

_____

_____

_____

_____

_____

_____

_____

_____

_____

_____

_____

_____

_____

_____

Day 19

"And my God shall supply all your need according to His riches in glory by Christ Jesus"

Philippians 4:19

Just do it

"All the people from countries came to Egypt to buy grain because the famine was great upon the Earth." (Genesis 41:57) Joseph was in charge of the largest storehouse of food, and supply ever recorded. God placed Joseph in the position of supplier, to give out the grain to the people as needed, for the famine was to last years, and the people came from afar.

We all come from afar places in our own lives. Places of loneliness, brokenness, betrayal. A feeling without hope or a future. Jesus gives us the food that our spirits, and souls so desperately need. Without it, we cannot survive. We have to go to the supply.

Joseph was a shadow of Jesus, for he supplied all the people needs. We have a much greater supply in Jesus, for the Word says, "My God shall supply all your needs according to His riches in glory in Christ Jesus." (Phil 4:19) The famine in the land was only an indication of the condition of man's heart. Are you in a famine? Are you putting God first? When we don't put God first in our lives making Him the source of our nourishment, we become spiritually famished. He MUST be first. Pharaoh said to the people, "Go to Joseph; what he says to do, do it." (Genesis 41:55) Mary on the day of Jesus' first miracle said, "Whatever He says to do, do it." (John 2:5) Mary wasn't even aware that her words would be an order for all mankind to follow. "Whatever He says to do, do it."

We as believers, have been given the commission to go out and preach the gospel. (Matthew 28) When we witness about Jesus, we are giving out The Bread of life, the truth. When He comes to live in us, we become the hands, and feet of Jesus. We hold the life sustaining bread that fed the multitudes. (Mark 6:31-44) We hold the source that fed manna to the Israelites in the desert. When Jesus told the men at the wedding to fill the barrels to the brim with water, He was indicating to us, that we will be, and must be, filled to the brim with the new wine that He was bringing. The wine that was served first at the wedding was the old covenant, and best wine was Jesus. (John 2:1-11) The new covenant that fills you to the brim with the power that comes when the Holy Spirit fills you to the overflow. Jesus is our supply and multiplier, and His supply will never run out, so we must share it. Let the Holy Spirit move you, and give you the words in your mouth to be the conduit to bring others to a life of peace, and freedom in Christ Jesus.

Day 19

"Now may He who supplies seed to the sower, and bread for food, supply and multiply the seed you have sown and increase the fruits of your righteousness."

2 Corinthians 9:10

Who are you going to share your supply with?

_____

_____

_____

_____

_____

_____

_____

_____

_____

_____

_____

_____

_____

_____

_____

_____

_____

Day 20

"Instead of your shame you shall have double honor, and instead of confusion shall rejoice in their portion. Therefore in their land they shall possess double everlasting joy shall be theirs."

Isaiah 61:7

What will your past say?

There is so much to be learned from the past. Archeologists continue to uncover the hidden mysteries of the ancient world. What were the people like? How did they live? What did they have at their disposal to build their settlements? Scientists learn so much by what was left behind. Remnants of walls built by man's own effort, and strength. Pottery that was used in the everyday workings of life. What will we leave behind for future generations to find? Our past is our story. What will your story tell?

Much of our everyday life is mundane work. Get up, go to work, doing the same thing day in, and day out. Come home, go to bed, and do it again. Routine can cause people to become complacent, and stop looking for the blessings that come in the little things. So much of what scientists find in an archeological dig, are the little things. But, little things reveal so much. It's a little thing that we get up every morning to go to the bathroom to brush our teeth, walk to the kitchen smelling the fresh brewed coffee, and maybe a bagel before work, but to many who don't have a house to live in, coffee to drink, a bagel, or any hope of food for the day, it's not such a little thing.

Perhaps you have lived a life that kind of feels like ancient ruins of devastation, and destruction. Maybe it wasn't a good childhood, but one of abuse or loneliness. God knows your hurt. God is not unaware of what you have gone through, or what you are going through. (Jeremiah 1:1) He said He will never leave you nor forsake you. (Deut 31:8) He bottles up every tear you cry. (Psalm 56:8) That's a God of love. If you open up your heart to Him, He will give you an ornament of beauty, instead of ashes, the oil of joy, instead of mourning. (Isaiah 61:3) The word says, "and they shall rebuild the ancient ruins; they shall raise up the former desolations and renew the ruined cities, the devastations of many generations." (Isaiah 61:4) Trust God to come in, and make all the ruins of your life beautiful. Look closely. See the little things He is doing in your life. As you give out praise, worship, and thanksgiving to Him, He multiplies back to you the healing of your past, healing of your body, and healing of your mind.

What will future generations find in your story, in your archeological dig? May they find a life of joy, and peace. A life of wholeness, one of worship, made and crafted, molded by the hand of loving God.

Day 20

"Thus says the Lord God: "On the day that I cleanse you from all your iniquities,
I will also enable you to dwell in the cities, and the ruins shall be rebuilt."
Ezekiel 36:33

What are the little things that you are leaving behind that will show you are a child of the Most High?

_____

_____

_____

_____

_____

_____

_____

_____

_____

_____

_____

_____

_____

_____

_____

_____

_____

_____

Day 21

"But certainly God has heard me. He has given heed to the voice of my prayer."

Psalm 66:19

A servant's heart

What was in Samson that defied God? What was the victory that was not fulfilled because of his rebellion, and complacency to the call of God on his life? Samson was a man called, chosen from birth for the time, and purpose to render the Philistines from the land. Samson disregarded the plan that God had in store for him, and went the way of worldly flesh. (See Judges 13-16) God even gave him unusual strength. He could rip apart a lion, and had the wisdom to tie fire to foxes tails to burn out the Philistines camps. But the problem Samson had, he wanted to do things his own way. He was self centered, and did things for his own gain. When we turn our eyes upon ourselves, and cannot see what God has planned for us, we then become a pawn of the evil one. God cannot get glory from selfish gain.

When we look out from ourselves to others, and declare "What can I do for you," that is when we are most like Jesus. Jesus didn't come to have people lift Him up, and serve Him; He came to be a servant. (Luke 22:27) He came to bring life, and life abundantly to those that are sick, and oppressed. (Matthew 11:28-30) Jesus came to set free those that are held captive by their own selfish means. We must look inside ourselves, and see if we are living a servant life, or one that asks, "What can I get out of this?"

Samson, on his last day of life, finally found the God he was to serve, and asked for the final moment to be used to bring glory to Him. Samson prayed, "O Lord God remember me, I pray thee, and strengthen me." (Judges 16:28) He cried out to the one who called him from the womb, and God was faithful to the cry. In his death he killed more Philistines in one moment than in his whole lifetime.

Look inside yourself and examine the inner thoughts and feelings that you have. Psalm 139: 23-24 says, "Search me, O God, and know my heart; try me and know my anxieties; and see if there is any wicked way in me and lead me in the way everlasting."

"If they obey and serve Him, they shall spend their days in prosperity, and their years in pleasures."

Job 36:11

What are you doing, or will do to show a servants heart?

_____

_____

_____

_____

_____

_____

_____

_____

_____

_____

_____

_____

_____

_____

_____

_____

_____

_____

_____

_____

"These all died in faith, not having received the promises, but having sent them afar off, and were persuaded of them, and embraced them, and confessed that they were strangers and pilgrims on the Earth."

Hebrews 11:13

By Faith

"By faith Noah, being warned by God of things not yet seen, prepared an ark to save his family. By faith, Sarah herself received physical power to conceive a child even after the age for it. By faith, Joseph when dying, referred to the departure of the Israelites out of Egypt."

Hebrews 11 reiterates a litany of people throughout the Bible of men and women who put their trust, and faith in God to see the miraculous happen in their lives. Many walked with the faith of a hope, and a future reward, not all seeing the tangible fulfillment of God's promises on this Earth. They looked at it as in a distance acknowledging they were only here on the earth for a time, and then comes the fulfillment of their promise.

What is the promise from God that they longed for? What did they keep striving for that carried them through some of the most difficult of times, and circumstances that we can't even imagine? It's the promise of a life to come. It's the promise of a heavenly home. By faith, Moses stood fast against Pharaoh, held his purpose, and led the Israelites out of Egypt to the Red sea, only to exercise, by faith, the crossing of it on dry ground. (Exodus 14) The Israelites walked seven times around Jericho, silently, wondering what God was doing, but in a moment God commanded, "Let the trumpets sound, and your voices roar for I have given you the city," and by faith, the walls of Jericho fell. (Joshua 6:1) Faith is seeing something done, but not having the tangible evidence of it now. (Hebrews 11:1) We all, even believers, walk through this life with circumstances and situations that have us all wondering at times, "What is God doing?" but through the hardships, through the pain, we have faith that there are better days. We have faith that God is working on our behalf. We have a hope and future reward.

Day 22
"The just shall live by faith"
Habakkuk 2:4

This time on Earth is so temporal. We must live each day looking to the day when He calls us to the heavens, living with a hope, and longing for the time of His appearing, watching the sky with our spiritual eyes living each day as a journey. The end promise is a wonderful goal, but; what if walking by faith in the God who brings you through every situation, sustaining you, prospering you, opening your eyes to truths of a promise yet fulfilled, is the goal all along? To walk with Jesus. To hear the Holy Spirit speak to you. To know God's character, and ultimately His will for your life. All the while, living by faith for the promise, 'yearning, and aspiring to a better, and more desirable country, that is a heavenly one." Jesus said, "I go away to prepare a place for you." It is only by faith do we see the end from the beginning. In our every day situations, and our eternal heavenly home.

What does faith mean to you, and what are some of your goals that you are believing by faith for?

_____

_____

_____

_____

_____

_____

_____

_____

_____

_____

_____

_____

"At midnight, I will rise to give thanks to You because of Your righteous ordinances."

Psalms 119:62

The Midnight Cry

The Ammonites were coming out against Israel just at a time of transition. Saul, was about to become king. Israel had never had a king before. So he was tried. The army was divided into three companies, and arrayed in the night. (1 Samuel 11-20)

It's midnight, and Paul and Silas have been beaten, and chained to a wall in the inner most prison. (Acts 16:16-40) But what is it that can be heard; songs of praise. Paul, and Silas were praising God in the middle of their circumstances. The earth shook ,and the chains were broken. Were they still in their midnight? Yes. But the chains that bound them had fallen away. Were they still going to have to face the prison guard? Yes. But a change had happened. The chains were broken, they were free. Victory in their spirits was the factor to their release as they praised the God of the universe.

Friends, what is your midnight? What darkness do you walk with today? God would say to you, "My mercies are new every morning. Put aside the weight you carry, let Me carry your load. Don't hide among the baggage you carry, thinking you can't do this, it's too big for you. You are more than a conqueror through Christ who strengthens you. "I will strengthen you, I will lift you up with my righteous right arm." says the Lord.

When Saul went out to fight the battle against the Ammonites, he didn't just go with three companies of men, He went out with the God who goes before you to fight your battles if you trust Him. God brought him victory that day. Who exactly was Saul? He wasn't anybody special. He was found hiding among the baggage when they went to anoint him king. He didn't have the confidence in himself to be king, but its not a confidence in ourselves that we are to rely on, we are to rely on the God who saves. The God who delivers. The God that breaks the chains that bind us. Don't fight your battles alone, fight with the name that is above every other name, the name of Jesus; the blood of the lamb, and the sword of the spirit, which is the word of God.

Fight the good fight of faith, lay hold on eternal life, to which you were also called, and have confessed the good confession in the presence of many witnesses. "

1 Timothy 6:12

Remember that you too have a company of three like Saul that fights for you. Let Jehovah Saboth (the Lord of Armies), Jesus Immanuel (God with us), and the Holy Spirit who is the power of the Most High (El Elyon) fight for you. Let Him be the light that goes before you, the One who makes your crooked paths straight, the One who lifts you up, and sets you upon the solid rock of Jesus, that doesn't sink or slide. Let the three in one be your saving guide, and watch the chains be broken off you, and freedom come to you even in the darkest hours. "For weeping may endure for the night. But joy comes in the morning."

Write a praise to the Lord

_____

_____

_____

_____

_____

_____

_____

_____

_____

_____

_____

_____

_____

Day 24

"Evening and morning, and at noon, will I pray, and cry aloud: and He shall hear my voice."

Psalms 55: 17

His mercies are new every morning

"I anticipated the dawning of the morning and cried; I hoped in your word. My eyes anticipate the night watches and I am awake before the cry of the watchman, that I may meditate on your word. My voice you will hear in the morning. In the morning I direct my prayer and look up." (Psalm 119:147-148)

There is such a hope in the new morning. Such possibilities lie ahead. All of creation coming into view as we see the glorious work of the Father's hands. Friends, whatever it is that you face in your life, God's mercies are new every morning. (Lamentations 2:22-23) Each day brings a hope of better things to come. God says to us in His word," Because he has set his love upon Me, therefore will I deliver him; I will set him on high, because he knows My name. He shall call upon Me, and I will answer him; I will be with him in trouble, I will deliver him and honor him. With long life will I satisfy him, and show him My salvation." (Psalm 91)

I ask, can there be a better promise? God knows what you face, what you think, what you feel. He is merciful, gracious, and loving.

As the sun rises, dispelling the darkness, put your hope each day in God. Jesus came as the light, and the light shone in the darkness, and the darkness could not overpower it." (John 1:5) If you keep yourself under the shadow of the Almighty, nothing in your day can overpower you; for you are a child of God, a child of the Light. So go about your day letting your light shine, so others may see the light and be drawn to the God that dispels the darkness.

Cause me to hear thy lovingkindness in the morning; for in You do I trust; cause me to know the way in which I should walk; for I lift up my soul to You."

Psalms 143:8

When you wake in the morning, what is the first thing that you think of? What sort of things will you say to God tomorrow morning as you rise to meet the day?

_____

_____

_____

_____

_____

_____

_____

_____

_____

_____

_____

_____

_____

_____

_____

_____

_____

_____

"He turns a wilderness into pools of water, and dry land into watersprings."

Psalms 107:35

Don't give up

"David was in the wilderness of Ziph, in the woods, and Jonathan, Saul's son, rose and went into the wood to David, and strengthened his hand in God. He said to him, 'Fear not, the hand of Saul my father shall not find you. You shall be King over Israel, and I shall be next to you. Saul my father knows that too." (1 Samuel 23: 16) David was being hunted by Saul. Why? What had he done that caused Saul to be so angry with him?

Sometimes, things in life are not of our own making, but out of our control. A sickness, an unexpected bill that you don't have the funds for, or maybe a person has betrayed you. Are you in a wilderness, with situations so strong against you that it feels like you might die if God doesn't do something? Is the oppression against you so fierce you are wanting to give up? That's just where David was. Saul pursued David to kill him. Jonathan came into the wilderness to strengthen David's faith in God, so he could stand against the attacks of Saul, Jonathan's father. Just like Jonathan, Jesus is there to strengthen you.

When we find ourselves in a wilderness period, we should take the time to seek, and reflect; "How did I get here?" Is there something I did that caused this? Could I have taken a different direction that would not have led me here? My friends, if you have the Holy Spirit inside of you, you have a direct compass to light your way. Take time in this season, and talk to the Father. Ask Him to reveal to you what it is He would have you to do. I guarantee He will be there to enlighten you. The Holy Spirit is our comforter when things het hard. He is our strengthener when the wilderness is overwhelming.

David was in the wilderness of Ziph, a city in Judah. You my friend, are in the hands of the Lion of the tribe of Judah. If you put your whole trust in Him, knowing that He is working all things for your good, He will lead you beside still waters, and make you to lie down in green pastures. Stand still, seek the help that can only come from the Lord. Watch Him light the path for your feet, as you see the wilderness clearing before you.

"For who is God except the Lord? And who is a rock, except our God? God is

my strength and power"

2Samuel 22:32-33

Write some scriptures that you can meditate on as God is bringing you out of
the season that you find yourself in.

_____

_____

_____

_____

_____

_____

_____

_____

_____

_____

_____

_____

_____

_____

_____

_____

_____

_____

_____

_____

_____

_____

Day 26

"Do not say, "I will do to him just as he has done to me; I will render to the man according to his work."

Proverb 24:29

Facebook generation

In today's time of Facebook, and Twitter, its far too easy to put someone on "Blast" when they say something about you that isn't true, or perhaps is, but you don't want the whole world to know it. In these times of social media, people don't have to look other people in the face when they say things about them. They don't even have to know them. Peoples opinions are out there for the world to see, and comment on. Feelings get very hurt. Sometimes, emotions are so high that a person will, or think about committing suicide. There are no immediate repercussions for them that want to "speak their mind."

David was in the wilderness. Pursued by King Saul out of his jealousy for him. Time and again, Saul tried to kill David. (1Samuel 23) Why? Because he felt inferior to him. The people liked David more it seemed. Do you see the similarities of today's climate of Facebook and Twitter? They said this about me, so now I am getting hate mail. They didn't "Like" what I said, so I am going to go after them, and make them sorry. But in David's time, the repercussions were more physical in nature. Not in a post where no one can get to you, but in real life; in your face where you may be dead in a moment kind of rage. Several times God placed Saul in the hands of David, only to have David stay his hand, and not touch him. David was right in the eyes of God. God said, "Vengeance is mine."

When people come after you, on social media, do as Jesus did when standing before Pilate. "He reviled them not." (Matthew 27) Keep your peace, and let God do the fighting for you. Don't speak evil of anyone for you know not the state of the heart of that person. Be to them an example. Show love to those who hate you, who speak ill of you. Forgive them, for God said, "If you don't forgive others their trespasses, then I won't forgive you, your trespasses." (Matthew 6:14-15)

David had much to be angry about. Run out of his home, fleeing constantly for cave to cave, staying in the wilderness to keep from being killed. But God was with David. He grew in strength and faithfulness to God as he humbled himself, forgiving his enemies.

54

"Bless those that curse you, and pray for those who spitefully use you."
Luke 6:28

Bless them and do not curse them. When you hold your peace, then the peace, and love that you show them will come back to you, as the hate will return back to them. Proverbs 26:27 says, "Whoever digs a pit (for another man's feet), shall fall into it himself, and he who rolls a stone it will return upon him."

Write some scriptures of peace to meditate on when people are coming against you.

_____

_____

_____

_____

_____

_____

_____

_____

_____

_____

_____

_____

_____

_____

_____

_____

_____

_____

_____

"As in water face answers and reflects face, so the heart of man to man."

Proverbs 27:19

Mirror Mirror

What do you see in the mirror? Do people see Jesus in you? Can they tell just after a few minutes of talking to you that you are a Christian? Are you a reflection of the love of Jesus?

A person asked an acquaintance of my husband, if my husband was still not drinking. The acquaintance replied, "Yes! He doesn't smoke, cuss, or anything anymore. Goes to church all the time." At the time this discussion took place, my husband had renewed his life with Christ almost 5 years before. People from his past were still curious if he was still straight. Like they were watching him to see if the transformation they heard about was real. My husband had been what people would call, a professional drinker, and drug addict. But praise Jesus that is all behind him, and you will find him every Sunday morning opening the door of the church for people with a warm greeting. (As of this writing, 10 years and counting)

Many people start out their walk with God with so much hope and excitement. Full of mercy, and grace; ready to take on Satan. That is until the persecution comes; and the worldly cares, and distractions start to interfere with the time usually spent with the Lord. When things start to get a little hard, they fall back into the old patterns, and ways of doing things. They start to compromise.

When we give our hearts to Jesus and become a new creature, we have a heart transplant. The stony heart is taken out, while a new pliable one is replaced. One that God can mold, and shape into what He wants that person to be. Will persecution, and pressure come? You bet ya. Satan isn't going to give you up that easy. But we have a helper in the Holy Spirit. He will strengthen you each day to overcome, because "greater is He who lives in you, than he that lives in the world." (1John 4:4)We as believers are to be, uncompromising, reflecting the glory of God to the lost and dying world.

When you show love to people that are unlovable, you are more like Jesus than at any other time. The world needs to see real genuineness. People strong in their faith. Never wavering, speaking to the wind, and the waves type of people. Will you be that person?

"*Then I will give them one heart, and I will put a new spirit within them;, and take the stony heart out of their flesh, and give them an heart of flesh, that they may walk in My statutes and keep my judgements and do them*"

Ezekiel 11:19

A people that when someone is going through a situation, they come to them for help, and advise, because they have shown themselves to have Godly character. A person that is trustworthy, compassionate, and walking in integrity. Are you that person? Will you make a stand today and say, "Yes, Lord. I will be that person. I will go out, and reflect your light so others will draw near to you. I will not compromise my faith, I will show the love of God to the lost. Use me Lord."

Take a look in the mirror. What do you see? What ways can we reflect the love of God in peoples lives?

_____

_____

_____

_____

_____

_____

_____

_____

_____

_____

_____

_____

_____

"Therefore you are no longer a slave but a son, and if a son, then an heir of God through Christ."

Galatians 4:7

Who do you say you are?

"So Mephibosheth dwelt in Jerusalem for he ate continually at the king's table (even though) he was lame in both feet." (2 Samuel 5:6) "Who am I ? Who am I that you are mindful of me? I am but a servant, that you look upon a dead dog like me." Mephibosheth didn't know who he was. He had been told his whole life that he would never amount to anything. His feet assured him of that for he was crippled. He didn't recognize that he was a child of Saul, the King of Israel. But in God's way of thinking, there is nothing He can't use.

What do you say you are? What is there in you that keeps you from accomplishing great things for God? Have you have been told your whole life that you wont amount to much? Did you not have the breaks in life, such as an education to propel you forward in a workplace that is a conduit to prosperity? These are just a couple of the things in peoples lives that they believe hold them back from the best that God has in store for them. God would tell you today that it isn't who you think you say you are, it's who God knows you are. Mephibosheth didn't recognize who he was anymore, he was reminded by David that he was a child of a king, and as such, he honored him by having him eat at his table for the rest of his life.

Friends, eat at the Kings table. The table of Jesus Christ. Eat of the bread of life, and be nourished by the word. Let it renew your mind and tell you who you are. You are the son of the King of Kings, the Most High God. The creator of the heavens. You are the heir, and joint heir with Jesus. Take your place at the Lord's table, and feast on the Bread. As you study, and digest His word, you study, and digest the life of Jesus. Let it be life to your spirit, health to your navel, and marrow to your bones. Don't let another day go by not knowing who you are.

Stand up straight, and make your declaration. "I am a child of the King. I am the righteousness of God in Christ Jesus."

"Day 28
" You are My friends if you do whatever I command you."
John 15:14

Who do you say you are?

_____

_____

_____

_____

_____

_____

Now, who does God say you are?

_____

_____

_____

_____

_____

_____

_____

_____

_____

_____

_____

_____

"When the righteous are in authority, the people rejoice; but when the wicked beareth rule, the people mourn."

Proverbs 29:2

Take your place

King David was on the run to the wilderness once again. Fear of his son Absalom gripped him. Absalom was trying to steal the authority of the land by sitting in the gate; listening to the people as they came to speak to the king, and giving them advice. David was so far removed from God's presence at this time that when word came to him about the takeover by Absalom his son, he never even consulted God in what he should do; he ran. David had lost his confidence to overthrow the coup against his authority. (2 Samuel 15:13-23)

When believers don't keep their fellowship with God daily, they get lazy, and it cracks the door for Satan to move in, and try to take authority over their lives. (Genesis 4:7) We must be in constant fellowship with God to keep the authority that we gained at rebirth. We as believers, are children of the Most High God. We are heirs with Jesus Christ, and through His shed blood on the cross, we have all power, and authority over the world, the flesh, and the devil. But we must exercise that authority in order to keep it, and the full confidence of knowing that God will go before us to fight our battles. The word says in Proverbs 3:26, "For the Lord shall be thy confidence, and shall keep thy foot from being taken."

David was again in the wilderness, but sometimes, the wilderness is where we see God do His greatest works. It's in the wilderness that we start to seek God again to hear His voice. Moses was forty years on the back side of the wilderness when he came upon a burning bush. You are never too far from God that He can't get to you, and bring you back to who you are. After Absalom was killed, David again went, and took his place in the gate. He took back his authority, but at a price of lives, and confidence. I say to you today, Seek God. Don't let the word depart from your mouth, and don't let a day go without meditating on the word of God.

Take your place.

"For there is no authority except from God (by His permission, His sanction), and the authorities are appointed by God."

Romans 13:1

Take an inventory, are you sitting in your gate? Are you exercising your authority? If not, why? If you are, how?

_____

_____

_____

_____

_____

_____

_____

_____

_____

_____

_____

_____

_____

_____

_____

_____

_____

_____

_____

_____

_____

"At the command of the Lord, they remained encamped and at the command of the Lord they journeyed; they kept the charge of the Lord, at the command of the Lord by the hand of Moses"

Numbers 9: 23

It's time to move

The Israelites were in the desert wilderness, ever watchful for the moving of the cloud by day, and the pillar of fire by night. (Exodus 13:21) "It's time to move." God was again on the move, and they had to be ready in a moments notice to pack up the tents, the tabernacle, and the millions of people to go forth as one. They were following the leading of the Lord.

We also are to follow the prompting of the Holy Spirit. When God gives us instructions, we are to follow them without question, because many times the road isn't very clear ahead. It's a matter of trust. Often times, the things that God is having us to do are well beyond our capabilities. It's in those times that God is giving us the grace to perform what it is He is having us to do. He will never leave you without the means to get something done. He is for you, not against you.

We must be diligent to look for the signs that it's time to move. When Abraham left his homeland, and family, God didn't give him complete instructions, he just said "Go" and Abraham was faithful, and obedient to go. (Genesis 12:1) It is better to obey then to have to ask for forgiveness because you didn't do what God said to do and, now you are in a situation not of God's making.

What does that still small voice say to you? We are to be leaning in, listening to hear what the Holy Spirit has to say to us. We don't always see everything, but if God is for you, you know you cannot fail. If He says "Go", then go for He will make your way prosperous. He will give you strength for the day, and rest for the night. Be watchful. Be diligent to hear.

Day 30

"In all thy ways acknowledge Him, and He shall direct your paths."

Proverbs 3:6

Write down what you are hearing God tell you as you lean in to hear him.

_____

_____

_____

_____

_____

_____

_____

_____

_____

_____

_____

_____

_____

_____

_____

_____

"Most assuredly, I say to you, unless one is born of water and the Spirit, he cannot enter the kingdom of God."

John 3:5

Who is the Church

When the Scribes, and Pharisees saw that Jesus was eating, and drinking with tax collectors, and sinners, they became indignant, and asked, "Why does He eat, and drink with tax collectors, and notorious sinners?" Jesus hearing it said, "Those who are strong, and well have no need for a physician, but those who are sick. I came not to call the righteous to repentance, but sinners." (Mark 2:15-22)

Who, or what is the church? The church is made up of believers. If you are a believer in Jesus Christ, and know that He is the only son of God, you are part of the church. Romans 10:9 says, "If you confess with your mouth the Lord Jesus, and believe in your heart that God raised Jesus from the dead you will be saved." People oftentimes have this belief that you have to be in a church, in front of a pastor, and confess your sins openly, saying the sinners prayer to be saved. Did anyone in the Bible do that? No. As the word was presented to them, they believed in their hearts, and in that belief, they were saved. Now, it does say to confess with your mouth. So if you believe in Jesus, and speak out loud that "Yes, I do believe Jesus is the only son of God," and if you speak out loud, "Yes I do believe Jesus was raised from the dead," then you my beautiful friend are saved. We don't want to get into legalism by saying, "NO, you must say it this way." There are only two prerequisites to salvation, belief, and confession. When Peter was told by an angel to go to Cornelius's house, he went and presented the gospel, and he, and his household were saved. 1 Corinthians 15:11 says, "Therefore whether it were, or they, so we preach, and so you believe." Does it mention praying a formula prayer? No. Is it a good thing to confess openly? Yes, because Jesus died openly on the cross for you, so it is good and right for you to confess openly before men, so Jesus will know you aren't ashamed to be seen as a follower Him. That's the reason for public confession.

"Then said Jesus to those Jews which believed on Him, if ye continue in my word, then are ye my disciples indeed."

John 8:31

The people sitting in churches aren't perfect. Many want to be. Many are seeking God with their whole heart wanting to have all that God has promised for them. But sadly, still fall short sometimes. But that is the wonderful thing about grace. God knows we are human. He made us. He knows what you think, even before you do. Do you think that because you don't go to a physical building of worship that God doesn't know you? You would be sadly mistaken. Even if you aren't a follower of Jesus, He knows absolutely everything about you, and still loves you, just the way you are. So come! Just as you are. Jesus didn't come for perfect people, He came for you and me.

Write down your salvation experience as a witness and a confession to others.

_____

_____

_____

_____

_____

_____

_____

_____

_____

_____

_____

_____

_____

"The Lord is my rock, and my fortress, and my deliverer; my God, my strength, in whom I will trust; my buckler, and the horn of my salvation, my high tower."

Psalm 18:2

Bread of Life

"While they waited until it should become day, Paul entreated them all to take some food saying, "This is the fourteenth day that you have continuously been in suspense, and on the alert without food, having eaten nothing, so I urge you to take some food. It will give you strength for not a hair is to perish from the head of an of you." (Acts 27: 21-44)

They were in a tempest. Tossed about in the wind, and the waves. Raging against them as they tried to seek a shelter to stay. "Take some food," Paul told them. "You have been too long without food." Are you too long without food?" Have you sat down to the table that God has prepared for you, and partaken of the bread of life that God has prepared for you this day? Jesus when being confronted by Satan said, "Man shall not live by bread alone, but by every word that proceeds from the word of God." The word is our bread. God has prepared a table for you in the presence of your enemies. (Psalm 23:5) Pull up a chair and feast on it, for it is life to your spirit, health to your navel, and marrow to your bones. It renews your mind that your thoughts become agreeable to His will, and then your plans will be established, and succeed. (Proverbs 16:3) It is the living water that gets down into your inner most belly, and becomes the living water that quenches every fiery dart of Satan. (John 7:37-39) It's a lamp unto your feet, and a light unto your path. (Psalm 119:105) It goes before you to perform, never coming back to you void, but going and accomplishing all that you sent it to do. (Isaiah 55:11)

The Word was sent to earth to be born of man, to live among us, and show us the way of salvation that all men be saved, and live a life for the worship of our heavenly Father who has made a better way for all who call upon Him.

Day 32

"Give us this day our daily bread."

Matthew 6:11

"It's been fourteen days since you have eaten men. Eat so you will be strengthened." We must feast daily on the word of God so we have the strength to withstand the wind, and waves of daily life. He gives strength to all who pull up the chair in the presence of their enemies. So pull up the chair. Partake of the Bread of Life, pour out the oil and give thanks for He is good, and He does good, and He does all things for our good.

What are you feasting on in the morning?

_____

_____

_____

_____

_____

_____

_____

_____

_____

_____

_____

_____

_____

_____

_____

_____

_____

_____

_____

"To open their eyes, and to turn them from darkness to light, and from the power of Satan unto God, that they may receive forgiveness of sins, and inheritance among them which are sanctified by faith that sin in me."

Acts 26:18

Seek the gift of Jesus

Isaiah 53 speaks of Jesus in details of His suffering as it was already done. "He was bruised for our transgressions, He was bruised for our iniquities; the chastisement of our peace was upon Him; and be His stripes we are healed."

God is not limited by time, for He is time. When Isaiah was prophesying of Jesus some 700 years before His birth, he could not have known the power of the words that he was given to speak. He was being obedient to the call of God. Today some 2700 years later, we are still seeking the words that Isaiah spoke to the people in bondage, of a savior that would come, and set them free of their captivity. Hallelujah, we today have that savior living in us, and looking forward to a day when our Savior and King comes to take us with Him to our eternal heavenly home. The word does not have a time limit. "Heaven and Earth may pass away, but my word shall remain." (Matthew 24:35) The word of God is power, love, joy, and peace all wrapped up in the name that is above every other name; the name of Jesus Christ.

At the time of this writing, we are in the Christmas season where people are busy buying gifts for loved ones, and milling about enjoying the company of friends, and family. We must never forget, especially at this time of year, that Jesus was the ultimate gift to the world. "You shall find the baby wrapped in swaddling clothes, and lying in a manger." He was a wrapped gift to the world. When we seek the gift God gave us, we will find the savior of our own captivity. As we go about in either this season of Christmas, or any other season of the year, we should make sure to give a gift back to the giver. A gift of love to the unloved, and the unlovable; for we were all at one time, the unlovable. Yet He loved us so much, that He stretched out His arms on a cross to die for us.

"For there is one God, and one Mediator between God and men, the Man Christ Jesus: who gave Himself a ransom for all, to be testified in due time."

1 Timothy 2:5, 6

What are you doing for those that are unloved, and unlovable?

_____

_____

_____

_____

_____

_____

_____

_____

_____

_____

_____

_____

_____

_____

_____

_____

_____

_____

Just a word of encouragement

"It only takes one touch from the Master's hand and he was made whole."
(Mark 1:40-42)

Peter and John were going to the temple to pray when they were stopped; delayed from their plan by a man on a stretcher asking for a gift. He was in need. Peter and John, were not irritated by the interruption in their plans, they simply turned aside to look intently at the man and spoke, "Silver and gold I do not have, but what I do have I give to you. In the name of Jesus Christ of Nazareth, walk!" and the man went into the temple leaping and dancing for joy.
(Acts 3:6)

Oftentimes in our daily walk, we come across people who need so badly for someone to stop, and look intently at them because they are in need of something. People who are hurt, lonely, or in pain, just needing a word, or an acknowledgement from someone, to know that someone else cares. Many Christians today get caught up in the, head down, scrolling, cell phone in hand syndrome that plagues the world today. So caught up in their own agenda, hurrying through the day not taking time to look into the eyes of people passing by because they are too interested in who, or what is being said about who, or what on Facebook or Twitter. How are we to help others if even we won't look into the eyes of the hurt and dying, to let the Holy Spirit move us to walk over to them, maybe just to give a simple word of encouragement. "God loves you, and He has great plans for your life." Maybe just eye contact, and a warm smile is all that is needed, and it opens the door for the refreshing, comforting wind of the Holy spirit to flow into that person, and do His work in them. As believers, we must be willing to put aside our own agenda in order to be used by God.

Just as Peter and John were interrupted with their plans, God wants to interrupt us at times to use us. Will you be open to the interruption? Will you be willing to walk without cell phone syndrome to look into the eyes of people passing by in the chance that God can use you? Will you be willing to miss kickoff, or a get together with your family or friends to bring love to the lost or lonely? God told us all to go into the world... Will you?

Day 34

Jesus said to him, "if you can believe, all things are possible to him who believes."
Mark 9:23

What encouragement can you give today?

"And Elisha prayed, and said, "Lord, I pray, open his eyes that he may see."
Then the Lord opened the eyes of the young man, and he saw."
2 Kings 6:17

Mundane Work

As we draw closer to God, He comes to us oftentimes in the most unassuming, mundane times of our day. Doing laundry, washing floors, taking out the garbage or even feeding the animals.

As Gideon was threshing in the wine press, doing what he normally did, just trying to get the work done, the Angel of the Lord came to him with a calling. The Angel of the Lord had been under the tree watching Gideon, and I wonder how long The Angel of the Lord had been there maybe thinking, "How long before he notices that I am here?" (Judges 6:11) And then the Angel of the Lord revealed Himself to Gideon.

When we aren't open to the spirit in the mundane things that have to be done daily, we lose the powerful messages He is wanting to show us through them. We must be open to see and look for His hand in the smallest of details. He instructs us to do everything as unto the Lord. You never know what the Holy Spirit is wanting to reveal to you if you are just open to hear.

Holy Spirit, I pray our eyes be open to see Your presence in the everyday, mundane working of our lives. Open our ears to hear, as You reveal to us the plan you have for our lives. Fill us with the peace of knowing You are always with us, and You always hear us when we pray.

Day 35

"Open my eyes, that I may see Wonderous things from Your law."
Psalm 119:18

How have you seen the God in the everyday, mundane activities of daily living?

_____

_____

_____

_____

_____

_____

_____

_____

_____

_____

_____

_____

_____

_____

_____

_____

_____

_____

_____

_____

_____

_____

Day 36

"Turn at my rebuke; Surely I will pour out my spirit on you; I will make my words known to you."

Proverbs 1:23

Open my ears to hear

Do you seek peace? Do you seek rest? In the days of King Asa, all of Judah swore with all their hearts to follow after God and keep His commands. God said, "I will be found by you," and He was, when they searched for Him with there whole heart. Asa and all of Judah had peace and rest because they put Him first. (2 Chron 15:2)

God speaks to us every day in our hearts, "Search for Me, Seek Me, I will be found by you. I will show you great and mighty things you know not. I will reveal to you the secret mysteries. I will reveal myself to you." (Jeremiah 33:3) God created you to be in relationship with Him. He wants that fellowship with you. A heart to heart fellowship.

Each morning I rise before the rest of the house while it's still dark, just to tell God how much I love Him. How much I thank Him for all He has done for me. Then I sit at the dining table where my husband and I study the word, and I ask God, "Ok God, what have you got for me today? What are you going to show me in Your word? What hidden mysteries are you going to reveal to me? Open my ears to hear You," and He does. God wants you to seek Him. Not because He needs you, but because He know how much we need Him. His word says that, "The wise also will hear and increase in learning, and the person of understanding will acquire skill and attain to sound counsel (so that he may be able to steer his course rightly.) (Proverbs 1:5) The word also says, "I will keep in perfect peace him whose mind is staid on Me, because he trusts in Me." (Isaiah 26:3)

When we have sound council, we then can make the right choices for our life. When we now and study the word, it becomes a lamp to your feet. Wherever the lamp light shines, that's the direction you go. Just as the Israelites moved with the cloud by day, and the fire by night. The word goes before you to perform, and it keeps your feet from stumbling or slipping. It keeps you on the straight and narrow path all the while directing you.

Day 36

"How much better to get wisdom than gold! And to get understanding is to be chosen rather than silver."

Proverbs 16:16

Whatever you face today, the word has an answer for. Asa found peace in God through following His commands. How much more peace can we have, with the Holy Spirit residing on the inside of us. So get your bible, your coffee, or tea, or whatever you drink, set you some time without distractions to sit before the Lord and ask Him, "Ok God, what do you want to show me in your word today? What hidden mysteries do you want to reveal to me? Open my ears to hear."

Get alone with God. Write down what you feel the Lord is telling you.

_____

_____

_____

_____

_____

_____

_____

_____

_____

_____

_____

_____

_____

_____

"May He grant you according to your heart's desire, and fulfill all your purpose."

Psalm 20:4

It's about the world to come

Solomon was asked by God, "What can I give you?" His answer pleased God. "Wisdom" is what he asked for. "how do I judge these your people?" God said to him, "because you have not asked for riches, or long life, I will give you these things also." (2 Chron 1:11-12) Solomon had anything, and everything his heart desired. He had wealth beyond measure. Wisdom so much in abundance, that people sought him out just to hear what he had to say.

With his wealth, he accumulated so many horses and chariots, that he had cities, and store houses built to house them and all the men to care for them. Gold and silver was so abundant that it was almost worthless. But; beware of all that you have in your hands, because when much is given, much is required.

Solomon took many wives from different lands. One wife was the pharaoh's daughter from Egypt. With many wives came many customs, gods and rituals. God says, "You shall have no other gods besides Me." (Exodus 20:3) Solomon was swayed from God by his wanting to please his wives. He slowly faded into compromise. Compromise brings rebellion, and with the wealth that Solomon had, it also brought pride. Even the accumulation of the worlds best horses from Egypt was a matter of pride. Deuteronomy 17:16 says, "he shall not multiply horses to himself or cause the people to return to Egypt in order to multiply horses, since the Lord said to you, You shall never return that way." But Solomon wanted them, so he got them. Pride replaced his dependency on God. The word says. "Pride comes before a fall and a hasty spirit before destruction." It is impossible to have a close relationship with God, and walk in pride.

The word says, "If my people, who are called by My name shall humble themselves, and pray, and seek My face, and turn from their wicked ways; then I will hear from heaven and will forgive their sin, and will heal their land."(2 Chron 7:14) God wants a humble spirit. When you humble yourself to God, the creator of the universe, He will bring honor to you, and exalt you in due time. Proverbs says He brings grace to the humble.

"Lord, You have heard the desire of the humble; You will prepare their heart;
You will cause Your ear to hear."
Psalm 10:17

Humble yourself today under the loving hand of God. It's not about this world,
and the things of this world; it's about the world to come.

How might you be compromising, and what can you do today to change and
bring a humble and contrite spirit before God?

_____

_____

_____

_____

_____

_____

_____

_____

_____

_____

_____

_____

_____

_____

_____

_____

_____

_____

"Then they entered into a covenant to seek the Lord God of their fathers with all their heart and with all their soul"

2 Chronicles 15:12

"When we come into the land, bind this line of scarlet thread in the window…"(Joshua 2:18)

When Joshua sent the two men into the land of promise to spy it out before crossing the Jordan river, they came upon a woman named Rahab; a prostitute. The men of the land were seeking to kill them, so she hid them for the night, and served them food. Rahab was a believer in the one true God, in a land of many gods made by man. She knew of these people that had come to the doorpost of the land, and they had something that she wanted. "Show kindness to my father's house and give me a true token." She wanted the assurance that her family would be saved from destruction as the Israelites came in to possess the promised land from God.

That's where the scarlet thread comes in. As Rahab placed the scarlet thread in the window, one of the men said to her, "Whoever shall go out of the doors of this house into the street, his blood shall be upon his head." (Joshua 2:19) You see, if they remained in the protective covering of the scarlet thread, they would be saved. Oh how glorious our God is. We as believers, are to keep ourselves situated under the covering of the one scarlet thread; the blood of Jesus.

The blood of Jesus covers us with a protection, and a covenant that is unbreakable. As long as we keep our faith, and trust in the blood that was shed, the act of sacrifice, the ascension, and the overcoming of death, hell and the grave; all that Jesus provided for us, we will be saved. Just as in the time of the Passover in Egypt, when Moses had the Israelites to place blood over the doorposts of their homes as the death angel came through the land killing all the first born who did not have the blood, we are protected under the blood sacrifice of Jesus.

Rahab, although a prostitute, was used of God, and can be found in the lineage of our savior Jesus Christ. With the one scarlet thread her family was saved, and through the one sacrifice of Jesus on the cross, we all can be saved.

"Then they entered into a covenant to seek the Lord God of their fathers with all their heart and with all their soul"

2 Chronicles 15:12

What family members are you placing under the scarlet blood of Jesus?

_____

_____

_____

_____

_____

_____

_____

_____

_____

_____

_____

_____

_____

_____

_____

_____

_____

_____

_____

"As for God, His way is perfect; the word of the Lord is proven; He is a shield to all them that trust in Him."

2 Samuel 22:31

The Lord recompenses

"The Lord recompensed me according to my uprightness with Him; He compensated and benefited me according to the cleanness of my hands. For I have kept the ways of the Lord," (Psalm 18:20) David was a man of war. Blood had been spilled all throughout his service as king; but, he was a man after God's own heart.

David was a man of repentance. His hands were clean. Having clean hands, doesn't come from never seeing battles; clean hands come from trust and obedience to God. "What is it You want me to do Lord? Anything. I lay my life before you. Use me anyway You would have." As we meditate on the word, and let the word be the lamp to our feet, and meditations of our hearts; then with your faithfulness to the God of all creation, He will lift you up to a high and large place. David gave praise to God in all things. When he did wrong, even to the point of murdering Uriah to commit adultery with Bathsheba, he was still a man after God's own heart. When he saw his sin, he was quick to repent. Not just a "I am sorry Lord." But a full heartfelt, fall on the floor, forgive me Lord, I can't stand to be out of your presence type of repentance." When we walk with God daily, making Him our delight, then we will be a person of clean hands. That's when God can use that person to do great and mighty things. He doesn't want weak children who don't make waves. He wants warriors, who will stand up and say, "Even though my enemies be many, I will go and fight the good fight of faith, for greater is He who is in me, then He who is in the world."

We have the battle won through our trust, and faith in God, and the word of our testimony. When we believe on, and trust in the cleansing blood of Jesus, He washes away all our sin, all our impurities. Be a person of valor, honor, and righteousness. David said, "Therefore the Lord has recompensed me according to my righteousness, according to my cleanness in the Holy Spirit sight."

"As for me, I will call upon God; and the Lord shall save me."
Psalms 55:16

Let God recompense you my friend. Let the Holy Spirit guide you, and may your thoughts become agreeable to His will, so that your plans will be established and succeed.

What were you going through the last time you fell to your knees in repentance?

Is it time to again?

_____

_____

_____

_____

_____

_____

_____

_____

_____

_____

_____

_____

_____

_____

_____

_____

_____

If's and Then's

"Because you have not asked for riches and long life, I will give you all you asked and these also." (2 Chron 1:11-12) Solomon had just ascended to the throne, when God came to him and asked him a question. (Be aware that when asked a question by God, you should ponder the answer carefully.) "What shall I give you?" God said to Solomon. What would you have asked for, if God came to you and asked you what He could give you? Long life? Riches? Health? Solomon asked for wisdom to rule the people. That was a good answer, and God rewarded him for it by giving him all he asked for and more. Only if you follow after God and keep all His commands. The word says in Proverbs 3, "My son, forget not My law, but let your heart keep my commands. For length of days and years of life and tranquility shall they add to you."

With God, there is always an If to His blessings. If you will do this, I will do that. Conditions are set to see if we will humbly surrender our will, to do His. Proverbs 3 is full of God's promises. "Let not mercy and truth forsake thee; So shall you find favor and good understanding in the sight of God and man." If you do, I will do. We all have a part to play in our walk with God. Just as in all relationships on Earth, it is a give and take. If you have someone who is always taking from you, eventually there wont be a relationship anymore because you will get tired of always giving. It's a one sided relationship. With God it's never a one sided relationship. He says, "If you follow my commandments, I will give you long life. If you seek after wisdom, and direction form the Holy Spirit, I will make you walk in safety, and your foot will not stumble." (Proverbs 3)

Seeking after wisdom shows a heart that's not self seeking. The word says, "Wisdom is more precious than rubies; nothing you can wish for is to compare to her. Length of days in her right hand and in her left are riches and honor. Her ways are highways of pleasantness and all her paths are peace." Does it say we never go through trials? No it doesn't. But it does say that when you seek after wisdom, when you search for wisdom, when you "Lean not to your own understanding, but in all your ways acknowledge Him, He will direct your path. For the Lord will be your confidence firm and strong, and shall keep your foot from being caught."

"And I have filled him with the spirit of God, in wisdom, and in understanding, and in knowledge, and in all manner of workmanship."

Exodus 31:3

With promises like these, it doesn't matter what comes against you. We have the reassurance and confidence that when we seek after wisdom, we will have "paths of peace." So today, If you seek wisdom instead of riches or long life: He will do all these and more.

What is your answer? What if God came and asked you the same question He asked Solomon? "What can I give you?" Ponder your answer, and write what you have in your heart. What do you want God to give to you?

_____

_____

_____

_____

_____

_____

_____

_____

_____

_____

_____

_____

_____

_____

"He will feed His flock like a shepherd. He will gather the lambs in His arm."

Isaiah 40:11

Listen closely

"Go out and stand on the mount before the Lord, and behold the Lord passed by." (1 Kings 19:11-12) Elijah had just had the greatest sign and miracle to attest to God's greatness since Gideon destroyed a great army with only 300 men. The power of God's might was on display to change the hearts and minds of the people. The only thing is, it's not in the signs and miracles that change people, it's in the still small voice that speaks to the inner person that changes them.

Elijah was discouraged, fearful of what someone had said. A great man of God, full of faith, calling down fire from heaven, ran to a cave, fearful and depressed. God asked Elijah, "What are you doing here Elijah?" (1 Kings 19:9) God spoke to him, and told him to stand at the mouth of the cave. "A great wind rent the mounts and broke in pieces the rocks before the Lord, but the Lord was not in the wind. After the wind, an earthquake; but the Lord was not in the earthquake; After the earthquake, a fire; but the Lord was not in the fire; after the fire, a still small voice, "Elijah, what are you doing here?"

God can do great and mighty signs and wonders, but it's not in the display of might that causes hearts to turn back to God; it's the still small voice that tugs at the heartstrings that changes a person. Three times God showed His might, but He was not in it. Three days Jesus went to the grave, but He is not in it. Jesus was freeing the captives, just as the Holy Spirit, who had been promised from Jesus, was taking His role to draw people as the still small voice.

It's not about grandiose displays of your religion so others will see how religious you are like the Pharisees, it's the life you lead. It's the words you speak when someone is in need of a word of encouragement. Does He do miracles? Yes! Absolutely; but His greatest miracles are the ones that are done in the hearts of people as they surrender their lives to the still small voice that calls them to the alter of repentance. It's at these times at the alter of repentance that lives are changed, and eternity is opened a little wider for someone.

"Out of heaven He let you hear His voice, that He might instruct you; and and on earth He shewed you His great fire; and you heard His words out of the midst of the fire.

Deuteronomy 4:36

So like Elijah, who was discouraged, and fearful, when God came to him and asked, "What are you doing here?" God is asking you, "What are you doing here? Come to the alter. I will meet you there. I will wipe away the hurt. I will fill that place in your heart that needs healing. Lean on Me. Let My love wash you, for My yoke is easy, and My burden is light." Listen closely for that still small voice, and see the miraculous take place.

Listen closely; wait on God. What is He telling you?

_____

_____

_____

_____

_____

_____

_____

_____

_____

_____

_____

_____

_____

_____

"Therefore if anyone cleanses himself ...will be a vessel for honor, sanctified and useful for the Master, prepared for every good work."

2 Timothy 2:21

Victory over the flesh

Jehoshaphat and Joram went to fight against the Moabite king. The Lord was with Jehoshaphat, but not with Joram for he served other gods. (2 Kings 3:7-10) Elisha declared victory that day because of the faithfulness of Jehoshaphat. The army came up against the Moabites and they slayed them as they went, and beat down the city walls.

It is interesting that as they went, the enemy was defeated. When we become new believers, or even if we have been in the faith for many years, we will overcome our enemies as we go with Jesus. Our sins are cleansed, our lives are changed, but in our flesh, it's time to go to war. Just as the kings destroyed the Moabites as they went, we too have to destroy our flesh and fleshly desires as we go about our walk with God. Things that have taken root in us, must be dug up and dealt with in order to live a free and victorious life in Christ. With the help of the Holy Spirit, the bondages that we all face will come to light, so that these things can be dealt with and conquered as we grow in faith.

My husband was a smoker. A big smoker. He dedicated his life back to the Lord on October 13, 2013. He knew the Lord was dealing with him about smoking, but he just couldn't put them down. He asked God to help him stop smoking, and God told him, when it was time, He would. Slowly he started to lay them aside, (notice I said he, my husband did) but the draw was still there. He was about to light up a cigarette on New Years Eve when he heard the voice inside of him say, "NOW!" and he threw the box of cigarettes in the fireplace, never to smoke again. The addiction was broken because he trusted the Lord to take them when it was time. He was obedient to throw them down and through that obedience, he was set free.

O sing unto the Lord a new song; for He hath done marvelous things; His right hand, and His holy arm, have gained Him the victory."

Psalm 98: 1

When we trust in God's word and His sufficiency in everything that He is dealing with us about, God's grace will see you through to the end. You will have victory over the flesh. What is it that you are dealing with? Alcohol, drugs, anger, bitterness, whatever it is, God knows what you think and how you feel. He knows everything about you, better than you know yourself. The word says that "He will never leave you nor forsake you." He wants you to live a life of love, joy, and peace. He wants you whole, so you can be a testimony of His goodness and help others to be set free from their roots of flesh; for in our flesh there is no good thing. BUT, we are the righteousness of God in Christ Jesus. We are heirs to the promise of Abraham.

So let the Holy Spirit reveal to you the things that may be hindering you, and like Jehoshaphat who slayed the enemies as they went, and tore down the walls, God will strengthen you, and give you victory over all that binds you.

What is God giving you the victory over?

_____

_____

_____

_____

_____

_____

_____

_____

_____

_____

"For the idols have speak delusion, the diviners envision lies, and tell false dreams; They comfort in vain. Therefore the people wend their way like sheep; They are in trouble because there is no shepherd."

Will you be the few?

"And they served idols. Of which the Lord had said to them, You shall not do this thing. And they did not fear the Lord but went the way of the nations." (2 Kings 17:41) We are a people that have been called by God to be a peculiar people. We are to be separate from the world.

When you meet someone for the first time, and speak to them for a few moments, can they tell that you are a Christian? Does your manner of speech tell them that you are different? What is it that you see everywhere you go, whether the grocery store, restaurant, clothing store, or gas stations? Cell phones. Heads bent down, no eye contact; no human interaction. Cell phones have become the modern day idol for multiple millions of people. Restaurants full of people scrolling on their phones across from other people not even engaging in conversation because they have to know what is being said on Facebook or Twitter. Not even a decade ago, people went to restaurants to have time together to talk. To interact. This world is losing the ability to interact as human to human. Then why do we not understand the increase of anger, frustration, and road rage. People don't know how to deal with their feelings anymore. There is no immediate consequence to what is said except by words on a computer. So when faced with an actual person in a situation that is difficult, anger and rage comes fuming out with very real consequences.

The word says we are to fear God and walk after His commands. Are you putting God first in your life? Are you taking that time to study His word and ask the Holy Spirit to help you to apply it to your life? Proverbs says, "He who keeps the commandment keeps his own life." The Israelites in 2 Kings, "feared the Lord, yet served their own gods,... they did secretly against their God things not right." They hardened their hearts to the Lord and they ere carried off, and many killed. Why? When they had the promise and the strength of God at their fingertips. When they repented, God was always there to fight their battles and give them victory.

"You shall not make idols for yourselves; neither a carved image nor a sacred pillar shall you rear up for yourselves; nor shall you set up an engraved stone in your land, to bow down to it; for I am the Lord your God"

Leviticus 26: 1

Today we have the Holy Spirit to guide us in our every day life. The word will speak to you, and instruct you in every manner of your day. Don't let the distractions of this world, the man made idols, keep you from your destiny with God; for the way is broad to destruction, but the way to life and eternal life, is narrow; and few are they that find it. Few! Let me ask you...

Will You Be The Few?

Look around you, what things in your life have become an idol? Pray that the Holy Spirit reveal to you what you must put aside. Then give God the glory for a life lived for Him.

_____

_____

_____

_____

_____

_____

_____

_____

_____

_____

_____

_____

"Go, and tell Hezekiah, Thus says the Lord, the God of David your father, I have heard your prayer, I have seen your tears; surely I will add to your days fifteen years."

Isaiah 38:5

Not my will

Sometimes when we are praying, we want so much for things to turn out the way we see them in our mind, but do we really know what's best for us? The word says, the "the way of man seems right to him but the end it lead to death." Hezekiah, upon his bed was told by Isaiah, "You will surly die." (Isaiah 38:1-21) Desperate times. Instead of praying to God for His will to be done, Hezekiah prayed, and pleaded for his life; as most would. He didn't know to pray, "Heal me Lord, but not my will, Yours be done." You see, he didn't know that in the next three years of his life a child would be born that would bring destruction, murder and heartache to the people of Israel. We as believers are to pray with a selfless prayer; What are you wanting Lord, above all else, what do you want to happen in this situation ? We are to rely explicitly on God. What are you believing for today that is a desperate situation? What are you pleading to God for? Are you praying for your will? Or His will?

So often times when we pray, we are not asking God to do His will, but to bless our plans. God's ways are so much higher than our ways, and His thoughts, so much higher than our thoughts,. He knows the end from the beginning and every minute detail in between. Does that mean we have no say in what happens? NO. There is a saying, "Be careful what you wish for, you just might get it." Hezekiah prayed for his life to be spared, and God granted his prayer. In death he would have been with God in heaven, so he would have been a winner there anyway, but in life, a child was born that would be a cause of so much destruction. Be careful with your life, the God who created you and everything around you knows what's best for you. It's not always the easiest road to take, but it will ultimately be the best road. We don't always know what tomorrow brings, or what consequences our decisions will bring. In times of desperation, persecution, circumstances beyond our control we want so badly to cry out to God and say, "I want it this way," but just as Jesus cried out for the cup to pass from Him as he pondered what was about to happen to Him on the cross, still He said, "Not my will, but yours be done."

"The Lord repay your work, and a full reward be given you by the lord God of Israel, under whose wings you have come for refuge."

Ruth 2:12

" He knew God had a plan for an outcome. Look at the surrounding circumstances with spiritual eyes, and set aside self, and say, "Not my will, but Yours be done," and God will go with you, walking you through to a right, good, and fitting conclusion, working all things together for your good.

It's a matter of trust.

As the words of the Garth Brooks song says, "I thank God for unanswered prayers." What have you asked for that you can look back at now, and say, "Thank you God for not granting that prayer."

_____

_____

_____

_____

_____

_____

_____

_____

_____

_____

_____

_____

_____

_____

_____

"But if from thence thou shalt seek the Lord they God, thou shalt find Him, if thou seek Him with all they heart and with all thy soul."

Deuteronomy 4:29

Seek Him and you shall find Him

"For there is nothing hidden except to be revealed, nor is anything kept secret except in order that it may be made known. If any man has ears to hear, let him be listening and let him perceive and comprehend." (Mark 4:22)

Jesus was explaining the parable of the sower and the seed to the disciples, but they were not understanding, for their spiritual ears were not opened to hear. (Matthew 13:1-9) Jesus was still with them, and the Holy Spirit had yet to come. Today there is so much word that is being preached night and day that there isn't a time that we aren't able to hear it. The word is ours to have, to seek, and to hide in our hearts. Jesus spoke in parables to distinguish between those who were sincere in their seeking of Him and the truth, and those who were only there for status, self, and power. The word says, "If you seek Me, you will find Me, when you search for Me with your whole heart." (Jeremiah 29:13) Jesus wants to be found by you. He wants to show you the mysteries and the things that you know not. Jesus also told the disciples, "Be careful what you are hearing for the measure (of thought and study) you give (to the truth you hear) will be (the measure of virtue and knowledge that comes back to you) and more besides will be given to him who hear." (Mark 4:24-28)

Are you listening for the voice of God? Are you sitting on the edge of your seat seeking Him and looking for what He is doing in your life? He said with what measure you seek, is the measure you will get. To those that seek with their whole heart, a fountain of blessings will be yours. What kind of blessings you ask? Love, Joy, Peace, Kindness, Patience, Health and Revelation, just to name a few. You will enjoy the fruit of the Spirit and they will be evident in your life. When all goes awry in your life and there are trials and tests, you my friend, can enjoy the peace that passes all understanding knowing that God is with you, and working all things together for your good. When you seek out the truths of His word, and let them change the inner man, you then become what God has intended for you to be. You are a child of the Most High God. You are an heir and joint heir with Jesus Christ.

"Direct my steps and direct by Your word: And let no iniquity have dominion over me."

Psalms 119:133

So seek Him, not for what He can do for you, Seek Him because He wants to be found by you, He wants to show you great and mighty things that you know not. He wants to be found. So when your time is done, and you enter the gates of heaven you can hear the words we all long to hear, "well done, my good and faithful servant. Enter into your rest,"

What are you seeking for?

_____

_____

_____

_____

_____

_____

_____

_____

_____

_____

_____

_____

_____

_____

_____

_____

_____

Day 46

"Surely God will not hear vanity, neither will the Almighty regard it."

Job 35:13

Vanity, Vanity

In a years time, Solomon received 666 talents of gold as taxes for all that he had built. Is it a coincidence that the amount of gold he received is the number of man's association with pride? Solomon asked God for wisdom instead of riches. God gave him both. Even with so much wisdom, Solomon went astray and was caught in the snare of mammon. Solomon had all his heart desired; gold, jewels, chariots, horses in abundance like never seen before, or since. But what was the cost he chose to pay for the extravagant life. Having everything his heart desired became a snare to him. He couldn't see the perfect will of God, he saw himself and his kingdom. (1 Kings 10:14)

The 666 talents he received in a year was his pride on display. Jesus said in Matthew in the parable of the talents, that the talent a person is given, if not dedicated to God, will be taken from him. Solomon didn't use his wisdom wisely.

The wives that Solomon chose were from heathen countries. He went outside the tribes of Israel, and with the wives from other countries came gods from other beliefs. In an attempt to please his many wives, he began to worship other gods.

Towards the end of a disillusioned, selfish, wayward traveled life, Solomon wrote the book of Ecclesiastes. "Vanity of vanities; all is vanity. What profit hath a man of all his labor which he taketh under the sun?" Solomon found that there is nothing beside God. All is vanity.

We must always look humbly to God and make sure our supply is used for God's kingdom and not selfish gain. Keep your eyes heavenward, that is where True Riches are stored. Jesus said it would be easier for a camel to go through the eye of a needle than for a rich man to enter the kingdom of God. Look to the example of Solomon, or the Pharisees. They were the head of the church in Jesus time but were so consumed with vanity, money and power, that they crucified Jesus in an attempt to not lose that power over the people.

"If My people, who are called by My name, will humble themselves, and pray, and seek My face, and turn from their wicked ways; then I will hear from heaven, and will forgive their sin, and heal their land."

2 Chronicles 7:14

We all must keep our eyes on the One who provides, not the provision. Walk humbly before Him. In due time, He will lift you up to a great and high place.

God is a good God. List the things that you are dedicating to Him, and thank Him every day for them.

_____

_____

_____

_____

_____

_____

_____

_____

_____

_____

_____

_____

_____

_____

"Wisdom is the principal thing; Therefore get wisdom, and in all your getting, get understanding."

Proverbs 4:7

Follow the instructions

"Let us bring the Ark of God to us, for we did not seek it during the days of Saul." (1 Chron 13:3) David was king, and there was peace. David sought the opinion of captains of thousands and said, "it seems good for me to do this thing", to bring the ark, and God's presence back to Jerusalem, and he proceeded to do it. The only problem was, he didn't ask God. He didn't consult the instruction book as to how to handle the Ark of God, and instead did it his own way.

When we walk through our life seemingly to do God's will but we don't ask Him if this is what we should be doing, many times it will end in disaster. Even if what we are doing is a noble thing, a good thing, a beneficial thing, if it isn't what God tells us to do, it probably won't meet with success. "Not My will, but yours be done." Read the instruction book; consult the instructor.

David got a new cart and had the Ark of God placed on it to bring it back to Jerusalem. When the ox stumbled, Uzza put out his hand to stabilize it and was struck dead. Fear came over the people. (2Samuel 6:1-7) David didn't consult God, or the instruction book as to how to move the Ark of God. Just like trying to put a piece of equipment together without the instruction book, you struggle. Pieces don't seem to fit. When you do though, the pieces are placed just where they need to be for success.

David didn't consult on how to care for the ark, thus it was placed in the home of Obed-Edom. The word says that his home was blessed for he cared well for the ark, and the presence of God. (2 Samuel 6:11-15)

When stepping onto the stage of life, look well to the instruction book. Seek the path that God has laid out for you. When we go out on our own without God's will being sought, it never fairs well in the end. "Lean not to your own understanding, acknowledge Me, and I will direct your path."

Have you ever put something together without the instructions only to have to take it apart and put it back together with the instructions? What do you need instruction in? What are you wanting God's guidance in? As you write, ask for the Holy Spirit to reveal to you the instructions.

"For thou, Lord, are good, and ready to forgive; and abundant in mercy to all those that call upon You."

Psalm 86:5

It's time to forgive

"Lord, how many times shall I forgive my brothers sin, till seven times?" Jesus replied to Peter," until seventy times seven." (Matthew 18:21-22) Forgiveness can be one of the hardest things for our flesh to do. Many times its people who are closest to us that have hurt or offended us that we must forgive. God said, "Forgive, or it will not be forgiven you." (Matthew 6:14-15) That right there can be a very scary proposition for someone who has been so deeply hurt that they have trouble just functioning in everyday life. God doesn't give you that command to help the person that hurt you, He gave you that command because He knows it's the only way you are going to be set free from the bondage of hurt and pain.

At the age of twenty four I received Jesus as my savior. At that time, God started working on me to forgive my father that was never there. Him and my mother divorced when I was four, and he was never truly in our lives. He was a part time to no time father. It wasn't easy to write the letter that the Holy Spirit prompted me to write telling him that I had forgiven him for not being the father that I had hoped he would be. Did it heal our relationship? Not really. It was another four years before I spoke to him. But I believe that God did a work that day, and started the journey to total forgiveness in me so I could accept the little relationship that we ended up having. I thank God for Him making me write that letter. It set me free from bitterness. I was able to look at him in another way. He was bound by alcohol and infidelity. I was able to feel compassion for a man that should have been their for me as I went through years of sickness, in and out of hospitals. God healed me. So I could bring healing to him through me forgiving him.

Did God want to send Jesus to the cross? No I don't believe so; but He did. Why? Because He knew that through pain comes true freedom. God uses the painful experiences you have gone through to heal you,. Doesn't make sense to our natural minds, but praise God, "His ways are higher than our ways and His thoughts are higher than our thoughts." (Isaiah 55:8-9)

"Now whom you forgive anything, I also forgive. For if indeed I have forgiven anything, I have forgiven that one for your sakes in the presence of Christ."

2 Corinthians 2: 10

As you draw upon the love of Jesus and the comfort that the Holy Spirit brings, you become strong. You start to overcome the hurt and pain that Satan wants so desperately to keep you bound with. Satan wants you to stay hurt so you don't move closer to God and realize who you are in Christ, and the plans for a destiny that God has for you. It's time to take back your life. It's time to make Jesus the focus of your faith instead of focusing on the hurt.

It's time to forgive.

As God is reminding you of what He has forgiven you for, write and pray about the people that you may need to forgive so you can be healed from hurt, and draw closer to God.

_____

_____

_____

_____

_____

_____

_____

_____

_____

_____

_____

_____

"The God of my strength, in Whom I will trust: My shield and the horn of my salvation, my stronghold and my refuge; My savior, You save me from violence."
2 Samuel 22:3

Fear Not

Jehoshaphat was before the great army of Edom. He cried out to God, "Will You not exercise judgement upon them? For we have no might to stand against this great company that is coming against us. We do not know what to do, but our eyes are upon You." (2 Chron 20:12)

Facing something so much bigger than himself, fear had taken over. Nowhere to turn but to God with a cry for help. The Spirit of the Lord came upon Jahaziel to tell Jehoshaphat, "Be not afraid or dismayed at this great multitude; for the battle is not yours, but God's. You shall not need to fight in this battle; take your positions, stand still, and see the deliverance of the Lord (who is) with you." (2 Chron 20:25) Just as God told Moses and the Israelites when their backs were to the Red Sea and pharaoh's army was closing in, God said, "Stand still and see the salvation of the Lord which He will work for you today." (Exodus 14:13) They put their faith and trust in God, and He delivered them from their enemies.

What enemies are you facing today? Whatever it is, know that God hears you. 1 John 5:14 says, "This is the confidence we have in approaching God: that if we ask anything according to His will, He hears us." What an awesome statement. "He hears us." It is such an assurance to those who feel they are in desperation. Calling out to God, "Help me!" Whatever the situation or circumstance that are facing, you can know He hears you and He tells you.

Often times we forget that we as believers are in a very real spiritual battle for our souls. The enemy comes against us to distract us and get us off course. He tries to keep us from fulfilling our destiny in God. We must remember what the word says, " For we wrestle not against flesh and blood, but against principalities, against powers, against the rulers of this world, against spiritual wickedness in high places." Satan wants you scared. He wants you to be in a position of fear and anxiety.

The only problem to that is; "Greater is He who is in us, than he that is in the world." Praise Jesus. He overcame the world so that we can live in victory over the world, the flesh and devil.

So when you feel like you are in a position of desperation, facing an army of circumstances too big to overcome; like Jehoshaphat, cry out to God and "Fear not, nor be dismayed; Go out against them, for the Lord is with you, the battle is not yours, but God's."

What battle are you trusting God to fight for you today? Give Him praise for it is finished.

_____

_____

_____

_____

_____

_____

_____

_____

_____

_____

_____

_____

_____

_____

_____

"Behold, the Lord's hand is not shortened, that it cannot save, nor His ear heavy that it cannot hear."

Isaiah 59: 1

What are you waiting for?

What are you wanting in your life? Is it wealth; prestige; or are you looking for something inside that you just can't put your finger on? A longing? An emptiness? Are you wanting to know peace; a real peace? One that lets you sleep at ease in the night. A peace where no anxiety lives. A peace that passes all understanding. That kind of peace that can fill all those empty places, and fills the heart with joy. It isn't a place, or a time in life; it's a person. His name is Jesus. The Prince of Peace, (Jehovah Shaloam).

Life takes a tole on people. Experiences that steal your joy. Death, health issues, abuse, alcohol, drugs, or maybe rejection. People will let you down. People are human, and humans are flawed. There is only one perfect human. God made flesh. Jesus.

Jesus came that you might have life, and life abundantly. (John 10:10) He came that you might have peace, not as the world gives, but a peace that passes all understanding. (John 14:27) A peace that when the enemy comes in like a flood, Jehovah Nissi will set up a standard against him.

Have you ever been to church and your heart just starts pounding out of your chest? Has the pastor given an alter call and you want so desperately to go down to the front but your feet are stuck to the floor? "What are people going to think? I have to get myself right first. They will think I'm a bad person. I don't want to embarrass myself." You are being called by the Holy Spirit. With all your flaws. With all your baggage. Of all the people in the world, He is calling you. He wants to come in and make a home in your heart. He created it and He wants so much to dwell in it.

People often think that giving their life to Jesus is giving up their life. That cannot be farther from the truth. The word of God is truth, and the truth will set you free.

"For God so loved the world, that He gave His only begotten Son, that whoever believes in Him should not perish but have everlasting life."

John 3:16

Free from sin. Free from anxiety. Free from loneliness, longing, emptiness. Freedom that brings a peace that whatever comes your way, you know that you have someone with you to help you. Jesus went to the cross and died, so that He could go to the Father to make intercessions for you day and night. He also sent the Holy Spirit to be a comforter, a guide to help you through your life. You are never alone. He knew you before you were even born. He knows your coming and your going. He knows every thought you ever had or ever will have; every action you have made, and still He calls you. Still He loves you. Still He wants to make you His home.

So what are you waiting for?

God gave His Son for you to be saved, what are you going to give to Him?

_____

_____

_____

_____

_____

_____

_____

_____

_____

_____

_____

"If you turn away your foot from the Sabbath, from doing your own pleasure on My holy day, and call the Sabbath a delight, the holy day of the Lord honorable, and honor Him and it, not going your own way or seeking or finding your own pleasure or speaking with you own words, then will you delight your self in the Lord, and I will make you to ride on the high places of the earth, and I will feed you with the heritage of Jacob your father: for the mouth of the Lord has spoken."

Isaiah 58: 13-14

Lord of the Sabbath

Sunday. Oh how I love Sunday. We get up, we get dressed in our best apparel and go to the house of the Lord. It is after all, the Sabbath day. Oh! Let me get my Bible from the shelf. Sunday's are the best aren't they! No work, no striving. Rest day.

Jesus said," Come unto Me all ye that labor and are heavy laden and I will give you rest." (Matthew 11:28-30) Does Sunday give you rest? No. It's just a day of the week. When we put our trust in Jesus, we make "Him" the Sabbath, giving us the rest we need daily from our life of striving and works. We are to honor Jesus "daily" by not going our own way, seeking to find our own pleasure, or speaking our own words, for the Word of God is to be continually on our lips. We are to meditate on the Word of God "daily."

Does that mean I don't have to go to church on Sunday because He is the Sabbath? No. The word says we are not to forsake the assembling of ourselves together. (Hebrews 10:25) It means that if you love Jesus with all your heart and soul, He will be Lord of "everyday". He will give you rest, "everyday". Unfortunately so many put Him on a shelf only to take Him down on Sunday. He wants to be Lord of every minute of your life. He wants to give you rest, peace, and joy as only He can.

Don't let another day go by striving to live life in a lost world without the only one who can give you the rest that you so desperately seek. "Seek ye first the kingdom of God" (Matthew 6:33) the Word says. When you do, "the peace of God which passes all understanding, will keep your hearts and minds through Christ Jesus." (Phil 4:7)

"Know ye not that ye are the temple of God, and that the Spirit of God dwelleth in you?"

1 Corinthians 3:16

What do you do on Sunday? What does the Sabbath day mean to you?

_____

_____

_____

_____

_____

_____

_____

_____

_____

_____

_____

_____

_____

_____

_____

_____

_____

_____

"For thou hast girded me with strength unto the battle: thou hast subdued under me those that rose up against me."

Psalms 18:39

The enemy cannot prevail

Moses and the Israelite people were facing Amelek. (Exodus 17: 8-13) They had not been out of Egypt long when the tests began to come. God had to see if they would trust Him in the trials. He had to see if they wouldn't run back to the land from which He had delivered them. How much of Egypt was still in them?

Moses, Aaron and Hur went to the top of the mountain to watch the fight, having the assurance that God was going to fight for them. Moses raised his staff. The same staff that brought them through the Red Sea. The same staff that struck the rock and brought water. There was authority in the staff raised high toward heaven. The battle raged and the Israelites were winning. But when Moses was tired and lowered his staff the enemy prevailed. Aaron and Hur seeing this happen, sat Moses on a rock, and held up the his hands and staff. The Israelites prevailed once again. As long as Moses's hands were in the air, they prevailed. But when lowered they were losing to the enemy.

(Exodus 17:12-14)

When we believers raise our hands in praise, we are giving our authority to Jesus. We surrender. "Not our will, but yours Lord be done". (Luke 22:42) Moses built an alter to God after the battle was finished and named it 'The Lord my Banner." Jehovah Nissi is our banner. When the enemy comes in like a flood, Jehovah Nissi will set His banner over you as a protective coat.

When we raise our hands in church to worship, we surrender. We surrender the authority over our lives to Jesus knowing that whatever situations or circumstances we are in or facing He is in the middle of them. So lift your hands to God in surrender and watch the battle unfold before you as He works all thing together for your good.

Day 52

"Thou hast also turned the edge of his sword, and hast not made him to stand in the battle."

Psalm 89:43

We all face battles at some time in our life. It's what we do when the battle comes.

Lift your hands, and write down what you are surrendering to Him today.

_____

_____

_____

_____

_____

_____

_____

_____

_____

_____

_____

_____

_____

_____

_____

_____

_____

_____

_____

It's time to rebuild

The Israelites had been taken into captivity because of their rebellion and idol worship. They had turned their back on God and in this state of captivity, Ezra found favor with God. Ezra was walking, and seeking after Him. He was allowed by King Artaxerxes to come before him with a petition. Ezra wanted to return to Jerusalem and rebuild the temple. It was time to return to where the people had left God. God's favor was on him to stand before the King, and he was granted that petition. (Ezra 1:1-6:22)

There are times as believers when we sometimes get off course. We aren't necessarily doing anything that would be considered sinning, but we are in a manner of unbelief, and rebellion. We haven't been keeping our hearts and minds under the umbrella (as Pastor Kym says), of protection. Sometimes our thoughts and circumstances of the day just get us off a little bit. You start thinking that it's not going to happen for you. God doesn't really have the plan for you like you thought. "How come when others pray they get their prayer answered, but I just seem to struggle all the time?" That my friend, is a line of thinking that gets you into unbelief, and unbelief gets you into rebellion. You start your trek into captivity.

Like Ezra, it's time to draw up close to God and trust Him. Ezra, even though he was apprehensive, prayed and fasted for three days before his journey back to Jerusalem. He was ashamed to go to the King and ask for soldiers to protect them after he bragged about how great God is. The word says, "So we fasted and besought our God for this, and He heard our entreaty." When you pray, believe that He hears you. Mark 11:24 says, "Whatever you pray, believe that you have it when you pray and it will be granted to you."

Ezra believed God, and it was granted to him. When you are out of sorts, go to the word. The Word is lamp to your feet and a light to your path. Trust that God is working all things for your good. Will it happen today, tomorrow or next year? Only God knows when the best time for your answer to be manifested into your life is. He knows you better than yourself.

"And he said, 'This will I do: I will pull down my barns, and build greater; and there will I bestow all my fruits and my goods'"

Luke 12:18

So like Ezra, go back to rebuild the temple of God, for You are the temple. You hold the presence and power of God within you. Just tap into that power; lift yourself up in your most holy faith, and rebuild.

Rebuild the temple. Who does God say you are?

_____

_____

_____

_____

_____

_____

_____

_____

_____

_____

_____

_____

_____

_____

_____

_____

_____

_____

"But if we walk in the light as He is in the light, we have fellowship with one another, and the blood of Jesus Christ His Son cleanses us from all sin."
1 John 1:7

It's time to move

The light flashed in a moment and Saul was blinded. Saul was having his encounter with Jesus that changes hearts and lives. "What do you desire me to do?" Saul asked, knowing that he had just met the Man, God, that he had been persecuting. "Arise and go into the city and you will be told what to do." Saul had been blinded by the light, physically and spiritually. He couldn't see so he had to trust the people that led him to the city, just as he had to trust the voice in the light that struck his heart. He didn't ask what was happening? He asked "What do you desire me to do? (Acts 9:1-19)

The order was clear. Go! The reason was not. In our lives we are many times instructed by God to go. Many times we don't know what the next, or even the first step is that He wants us to take; but we are to trust Him to move. We want so much to have the answers to our questions before we take the step of faith. We want to know why? And how? But much of the time it's just the act of obedience to move that gives way to a knowing in our heart what to do, and where to go.

God said in Jeremiah 29:11 "For I know the plans I have for you, plans for your well-being not for disaster to give you a hope and a future." When God moves, it's time to move. When the Israelites were in the wilderness, they had a cloud by day, and fire by night to know when God was on the move. Today we have the inner voice of the Holy Spirit. We must make ourselves available to hear His voice when He speaks and tells us, "Go".

Obedience and trust is the road that leads to a "Well done, good and faithful servant. Now enter the kingdom of heaven." Will you be obedient to His voice? Will you trust Him when He says move, even when you have no idea how it's going to get done?

Will you believe He is working all things for your good?

"You are all sons of light and sons of the day. We are not of the night nor of darkness."

1 Thessalonians 5:5

What has God laid on your heart to trust and be obedient about?

_____

_____

_____

_____

_____

_____

_____

_____

_____

_____

_____

_____

_____

_____

_____

_____

_____

_____

_____

"But let him ask in faith, with no doubting for he who doubts is like a wave of the sea driven and tossed by the wind."

James 1:6

Faith in patience

Thomas was not present when Jesus appeared to the disciples after He was crucified. Thomas refused to believe until he saw Jesus for himself, even though he walked with Jesus daily, and saw the miracles for himself. When the miracles stopped, so did his faith. (John:24-29) That is so indicative of peoples reactions today. When God is moving, and situations and circumstances are being resolved, it's easy to have to faith. But what about those times when the answers, the directions are slow in coming? You start thinking, "Why is it taking so long? I prayed! I believed." How are you going to respond in the times when God is silent?

In our walk with God, there are times when our faith is tested. It's time to see if you can walk out what you believe, and wait patiently for the answer or thing you are believing for. James 1:3-4 says "knowing this that the trying of your faith worketh patience. But let patience have her perfect work that ye may be perfect and entire, wanting nothing." It takes faith to believe for something, and patience to wait for it. The word says, "Faith is the substance of things hoped for, the evidence of things not seen."

Faith is like layaway. You have this beautiful item you are purchasing, and you make a down payment on it, knowing when it's paid it's yours. We put a down payment of faith on what we are believing for, and just like layaway, we continue to make payments of faith, believing that when the time is right we will have what we believed for.

Thomas believed in Jesus, but he didn't have the faith to see the unseen. Jesus said, "Blessed are those who believe but have not seen," So take what you are believing for, and put it on layaway. Put down your payment of faith, and keep making your payments of faith knowing that when the time is right, it's yours.

Day 55

"What does it profit my brethren, if someone says he has faith but does not have works?"

James 2:14

What do you have on layaway?

_____

_____

_____

_____

_____

_____

_____

_____

_____

_____

_____

_____

_____

_____

_____

_____

_____

_____

_____

_____

_____

"For she did not know that I gave her corn, and wine, and oil, and multiplied her silver and gold, which they prepared for Baal."

Hosea 2:8

She didn't know

Gomer didn't know. She didn't know the love of God. (Hosea) The love of a secure peaceful life that comes with a relationship with Him. Do you my friend have that relationship with Him? Do you spend time with God like He is your very best friend in all the world? Well that's exactly what He is wanting. That's exactly what He longed for from the people of Israel. He chose them as His own particular people. He gave them blessings, food from heaven, protection from surrounding armies; but unfortunately, they didn't have that kind of love back for Him. They rebelled. They did what they wanted to do, and followed after other gods.

That's where we find Gomer. God told Hosea (a righteous man) to go and marry a prostitute. (Hosea 1) Wow! Really! Why would a righteous loving God want to inflict such pain on a righteous man? He wasn't. He was teaching. Sometimes the hard lesson that we go through, is the correction process for which God is going to get the most glory. Hosea was to go and love Gomer as God loved Israel. Gomer had been so far from God she didn't know that the corn, wine and oil that she prepared for Baal came from God's provision. She didn't know. She wasn't in tune with the God that had chosen them to be His own.

Hosea loved Gomer even though she continued to play the harlot; even to the point of being sold as a slave for 15 pieces of silver, and 1 1/2 homers of barley. God was making a point to the people of their own rebellion. You know someone had to stop Hosea and ask him why he married Gomer, and continued to take her back when she ran off and prostituted herself. You can almost hear Hosea saying "So glad you asked...", and God's plan to reveal to the Israelite people their own rebellion was revealed through the example of unconditional love.

"Let us draw near to God with a sincere heart and with the full assurance that faith brings. Having our hearts sprinkled to cleanse us from a guilty conscience and having our bodies washed with pure water."

Hebrews 10:22

We too are Gomers at times. When the things of this world take precedence over God. When daily routine, work, sports, or social media become god instead of God. When you don't have time to fit in a bible study, reading the word, on your knees praying, or listening for the voice of God, but have all the time in the world to see what was posted on Twitter, or Facebook. Time to watch a four hour game of football or tennis. You have become a prostitute to this world.

You as believers, are chosen. When you turn your back and walk away, God woos you back. Turning you back from sin, time and again until you are fully invested in the marriage as His bride. If you find yourself in the Valley of Achor, turn back to Jesus, your first love, and do your first works over again. He will be there to take you in, and love you with all that He is, just like Hosea loved Gomer.

How can we be a service to others, building up each other to a more abundant exercise of love?

_____

_____

_____

_____

_____

_____

_____

_____

_____

Are you a Conie?

Psalms 104:18 says, "the rocks are a refuge for the conies." Charles Spurgeon talks of the conies and where they live as uninhabitable places. "The chamois (goat), leaps from crag to crag, and the conie burrows beneath the soil. For one creature the loftiness of the hills and for another, the hollowness of the rocks serves as protection: this all the Earth is full of happy life, every place has it's appropriate inhabitants, nothing is empty and void and waste."

Palms 104 is a wonderful expression of God's creation. Each creation day is represented showing His glorious power and greatness. Even the minutest of animals such as the conie finds it's way into the word of God.

The conies live among the rocks and hide there like a refuge. It is listed in proverbs among the exceedingly wise. Why? Why is this little animal no bigger than a mouse, listed among the wise? They find their home in the rock; hidden as a refuge. Psalms 91 says, "I will say of the Lord, He is my refuge and my fortress, my God; on Him will I lean on and rely, and in Him I trust."

Compared to God, we are but feeble folk. But when we are hidden in the rock of Jesus Christ, and when we rely on Him, and trust Him, we are then counted as amongst the wisest of creatures, seeking Him as a refuge from the snares of the world. We are to stand on the word of God, like Isaiah 55:11 says," So shall my word be that goes forth from my mouth; it shall not return to me void, but it shall accomplish that which I please, and it shall prosper in the thing to where I sent it," The word is power from the snares of the world.

So why does the author of Proverbs and Psalms tell us to consider the little Conie? Because he knew that even the littlest feeble folk who make their homes upon the Rock, have a refuge in the awesomeness of our Lord Jesus Christ, and we are sheltered from the enemy.

So meditate on this little feeble folk, whom God calls amongst the wisest of creatures.

Are you a Conie?

"For the Lord gives wisdom; from His mouth comes knowledge and understanding."
Proverbs 2:6

What choices have you made lately that would be considered wise?

_____

_____

_____

_____

_____

_____

_____

_____

_____

_____

_____

_____

_____

_____

_____

_____

_____

_____

_____

_____

_____

"I dwell in the high and holy place, with him who has a contrite and humble spirit, to revive the spirit of the humble, and to revive the heart of the contrite ones."

Isaiah 57:15

Correction in Love

King David was bringing the ark of the covenant back to Jerusalem after being in the hands of the Philistines for many years. A cart was built and the ark placed upon it for travel. Everyone was happy and joyful until the oxen stumbled, and Uzza reached out his hand to stabilize the ark on the cart, and God struck Uzza dead. (2 Samuel 6:1)

Why? Why did God strike him for helping to stabilize the ark? Disobedience. God had a specific plan for how the ark was to be cared for. The ark after all was the physical representation of His presence. King David was fearful, and sent the ark to stay in the home of Obed-Edom; and the word says, "the Lord blessed the house of Obed-Edom and all that he had." (2 Samuel 6:11-15) Why was his house blessed after God had struck Uzza dead because of the ark? Obed-Edom knew how to keep and care for the ark. He knew how to honor it. Like Joshua said to the Israelites, "As for me and my house, we will serve the Lord." (Joshua 24:15) Obed-Edom was saying the same thing. He knew there was a way to honor and keep God's presence.

King David sought and learned how to care for the ark properly, and when it was time to bring the ark to Jerusalem, there was dancing and worship that went before the ark, with the Levites caring for it as God had instructed. And who was one of the worshippers ; Obed-Edom. He played the harp and worshipped. When the ark was placed in the temple, Obed-Edom became a servant, and gatekeeper to the ark. He was faithful. He was humble. He was a worshipper, and he knew how to keep Gods presence. (2 Samuel 6:14-22)

When we go out and try to do things on our own, (even if it seems right) if it isn't the way God instructs, then we are out of His will and are being disobedient. There are consequences to disobedience and we must be corrected. The great thing about correction is, Proverbs 13:12 says, "For the Lord corrects those He loves, just as a father corrects a child in whom he delights."

"Do not forget the covenant I made with you. You must not worship other gods. You must worship only the Lord your God. He is the one who will rescue you from all your enemies."

2 Kings 17:38-39

You see, it is a sign of God's love to you when you are being corrected. Does it feel good? No! Correction never feels good, but in the correction, you learn truth. Jesus is the way, truth, and the life. You learn the way God wants you to live and move in your life. It's through correction that you draw closer to God. So come to Him, humble and contrite, with a grateful heart, for in His presence there is fullness of joy.

Where have you been disobedient to the Lord, and how can you change?

_____

_____

_____

_____

_____

_____

_____

_____

_____

_____

_____

_____

_____

_____

_____

"And who knows but that you have come to the kingdom for such a time as this and for this very occasion?"

Esther 4:14

And who knows

"In the days of Esther, King Ahauserus asked for the presence of Queen Vashti at the dinner party for kings. She refused. What was to be done? She would be put away and a new queen would be found. A search throughout the land was made for all the maids to come before the king to see who would become the next queen. " (Esther 1:10-22)

Esther was the niece of Mordecai the Jew. He raised her as his own. She was not only beautiful in appearance but also in spirit. She had been chosen for the preparation period to come before the king. In her humble spirit she asked the eunuch in charge of the harem what was best to have to go into the presence of the king for she had found favor with the eunuch. She did only what he said, and she was chosen among the land to be the next queen.

Haman was the second I command in the country. He hated the Jews. Especially Mordecai because he wouldn't bow to him. Mordecai at one time had saved the king from an evil plot to kill him but was never recognized. Haman tricked the king into making a proclamation to kill all the Jews. Mordecai had to get to Queen Esther. It was a dire time. Their lives were on the line. The king, unknowingly just signed his queen's death certificate.

Upon hearing the devastating news about the proclamation, Mordecai asked Queen Esther for help to go before the king. That was unheard of. People just don't go before the king. You are called. But Mordecai made sure Esther knew her position. "Do not flatter yourself that you shall escape in the king's palace any more than all the other Jews. For if you keep silent at this time, relief and deliverance shall arise for the Jews from elsewhere, but you and your father's house will perish. **And who knows but that you have come to the kingdom for such a time as this very occasion.?" (Esther 4:14-16)**A time of fasting and prayer was had to give Esther favor before the king. She came humbly before the king and found the favor she had prayed for, and in time, the evil plot to kill the king was revealed, Mordecai was honored before Haman, and Haman's plan to kill the Jews was made known and overturned.

"And He made from one all nations of men to settle on the face of the earth, having definitely determined their allotted periods of time and the fixed boundaries of their habitation."

Acts 17:26

We read about Esther and the plot twists and turns in her life. Nowhere in the book of Esther is God mentioned. Really? Nowhere? No. The book of Esther so beautifully shows us the providence of God. How nothing in our life is a coincidence. You see Haman would have had all the Jews killed if it wasn't that Esther was not queen. It wasn't a coincidence that she was there in the palace at that time. For Mordecai said to her, "Who knows but that you have come to the kingdom for such as time as this.

God works behind the scene in all of our lives. He moves things, people, situation, all around to make the end result that He needs at a specific time. When you think that something is a coincidence. Look closely. It just may be that you were called for such a time as this.

What coincidence in your life can you see the hand of God?

_____

_____

_____

_____

_____

_____

_____

_____

_____

_____

Day 60

"You keep him in perfect peace whose mind is stayed on You, because he trusts in You."

Isaiah 26:3

BUT GOD

I know that sometimes its very hard to give thanks especially where you are sitting right now. The apostle Paul was in prison when he wrote most of the books of the old testament. In 2Timothy 2:8, Paul writes, "For which I am suffering, bound with chains as a criminal. But the word of God is not bound." He was an innocent man; his only crime, preaching the gospel. In Acts 16:25 it reads, "About midnight Paul and Silas were praying and singing hymns to God, and prisoners were listening to them." Here they were, bound at the feet, with their arms shackled to the wall, in a very damp, dark dungeon of a prison. The inner prison; praising God and singing after having been beat with rods to bleeding.

We all have some sort of prison at times. For many of us, the prison is inside of us. Loneliness, depression, self-loathing, anger, addiction or even thoughts of suicide. You don't have to be in a literal prison to feel like you are. My husband dealt with depression for years. It was dark. Suicidal thoughts were prevalent. He didn't have a good childhood where his parents loved on him and cared for him. He was in the way. His parents were alcoholics. He was dropped at this house or that house just to be out of the way. He was alone, and as an adult he too became an alcoholic and a drug user. BUT GOD intervened and through prayer and meditating on the word of God he was able to overcome. He couldn't do it alone; he had to have the word working on the inside of him. He needed the word to renew his mind.

You see the mind is Satan's playground. He wants you to be depressed; always looking at the bad. I know for many of you, life has been rough, and adding to it some bad decisions. But you can start fresh and new. He cleanses and makes your life a new life. A life of hope and a future reward with Him in heaven. Will things change automatically when you believe? No not usually. BUT GOD will walk with you and teach you through His word how to overcome the enemies in your life. YOU CAN HAVE THE MIND OF CHRIST.

"Therefore be imitators of God, as beloved children."

Ephesians 5: 1

Romans 8:6 says, "For to set the mind on the flesh is death, but to set the mind on the Spirit is life and peace." Romans 12:2 says, "Do not be conformed to this world, but be transformed by the renewal of your mind." The word, when meditated on, renews the way you think. At one time you thought the world's way, and now you begin to thin God's way. And in Isaiah 26:3, the word says, "You keep him in perfect peace whose mind is stayed on You, because he trusts in You." The word is full of wonderful promises of God. They are ours for the taking, but you must believe and trust in the word of God. So determine today to read and meditate on the word. I promise you, the Holy Spirit will start the renewal process, and soon you wont even recognize the person you once were.

What is your prison?

_____

_____

_____

_____

_____

_____

_____

_____

_____

_____

_____

_____

_____

_____

_____

"Our Father in heaven, Hallowed be Your name. Your kingdom come. Your will be done on earth as it is in heaven. Give us day by day our daily bread. And forgive us our sins, For we also forgive everyone who is indebted to us. And do not lead us into temptation, but deliver us from the evil one."

Luke 11:2-4

The Lord's Prayer

Growing up a non-practicing Catholic, I learned this prayer to pray before I even knew what it was saying to me. I was to just learn it. Just pray it. So, I did. I got down on my knees every night before bed (drunk, high, it didn't matter) and I prayed this prayer and asked for protection through the next day. It was a matter of wrote. I just did it. Not really meaning what I said but doing it because I always did it. Was taught to do it. That is until I was invited to a very strange Pentecostal church and met Jesus at the alter and was transformed into a new creation. (2 Cor 5:17) As a non-practicing Catholic, I wasn't really taught to study the bible for myself, or to see what it was saying to me. But as a new creation, I had a hunger and a thirst for the word. And as I studied, low and behold the prayer that I had been praying since childhood (I don't even know how old I was when I started praying it) was right there on the pages of the bible. "WOW!!! Hey Gary! Look what's in the bible!" I yelled to my husband. I was floored. He laughed. Why hadn't anyone in the church told me I was praying the Word of God. How cool was that. (I was much younger and knew NOTHING about the word of God). I grew up in New Hampshire and was 14 when my family moved to Georgia. Not as many Pentecostal churches in the north. He on the other hand being born in the bible belt of the country, had heard the word from preaching when he went with friends to church occasionally. (I was again floored when we moved here how many people went to church on Sunday in the south even when their actions didn't reflect it during the week). I believe that the prayer that I had learned as a child, God honored, because of my ignorance of the Word. I didn't know. And because I didn't know, He honored it.

He knows the end from the beginning of every one of our lives and I believe He knew that when I was 24 years old, I was going to accept Him as my savior, and my life would be forever changed. (Of course, I did make a very 180 degree turn 16 years later at 40 years of age and started drinking and doing drugs. I went about as far from God as you can get without denying Him for almost 10 years. The scars I wear on my arms are my testimony of God's goodness in bringing me back to Him even when I turned away.) But the word changed what I thought, and in turn changed who I was, and then changed the direction I was headed in.

When you read the bible, the word says in **Proverbs 3:6-8**, **IF YOU**, "In ALL your ways know, recognize, and acknowledge Him, **HE WILL** direct and make straight your paths. Don't be impressed with your own wisdom. Instead, reverently fear the Lord and **turn (entirely) away from evil**. **Then** you will have healing for your body and strength for your bones." You see **IF YOU** accept Him, and acknowledge Him, **HE WILL** direct your paths. **IF YOU** turn from ALL evil, **HE WILL** give you health. Like the Lord's prayer says, **HE WILL** give you daily bread. **HE WILL** forgive you of your sins. **HE WILL** keep you from temptations and rescue you (and don't we know there are a lot of temptations in the world).

All the promises of God in the bible are yours **IF YOU** want them. **IF YOU** accept Him into your heart so you can be saved and become a new creation. **IF YOU** study the word, and **IF YOU** obey His word, **HE WILL** be all you need Him to be. **BUT ONLY IF YOU...**

Make it a daily habit to read the Lord's Prayer every day for 30 days and write down how it is changing you.

_____

_____

_____

_____

_____

"From there he went on toward the hills east of Bethel and pitched his tent, with Bethel on the west and ai on the east. There he built an alter to the Lord and called on the name of the Lord."

Genesis 12:8

The Road of Decision

All too often we must come up out of Egypt and go back to the place where we last heard God speak to us. Such was the place that Abram (Abraham) and Sarai (Sarah) found themselves in Genesis chapter 13. Abraham had heard from God to move away from his family and seperate himself to hear from God and let God guide him. So off he went. When he got to hear from God and let God guide him. So off he went. When he got to Bethel (which means house of God) he heard from god and built an alter there. News of a famine in the land caused him to fear so he took a turn and went to Egypt where he lied about who he was and almost brought disaster upon his wife and country. (Thankfully, God stopped that) and Abram left Egypt to go back to Bethel where he heard the voice of God to ask him which way to go.

Have you ever thought you knew which way to go in your life but something happened and you ended up going the wrong way? We all may have at one time or another. I was in church for 16 years. Devout and a follower of Christ raising my children. We stopped going to church (for reasons I wont go into) and that started us on a path of destruction. At first it seemed fine. I will only drink one beer. Oh! You got a joint, Ok it's harmless. Then before I knew it, 10 years later, my husband and I were full blown alcoholics and drug addicts. Our marriage was essentially over, and my 15 year old daughter had a baby. Was that a wrong direction if there ever was!

BUT GOD was gracious and merciful to draw us back to Him. He didn't leave us where we were because at one time we gave ourselves to Him and were saved. God is so merciful that when things get so bad you can't go forward or backward, He meets you right there. Right there in your sin to welcome you and bring you back to the last time where you had a decision to make deciding which path to go. Except this time, He will go with you.

Day 62

"The Israelites went up to Bethel and inquired of God."

Judges 20:18

Today my husband is a greeter at the church and is the person responsible for closing up the church after service. I also am a greeter for the children's church. We are blessed beyond measure because He brought us back out of our Egypt to Bethel. The House of God.

Let God direct you back to where you were at the fork in the road, having to make a crucial decision on your path to life, and He will lead you on paths of righteousness.

Write your paths down as you seek God for direction

_____

_____

_____

_____

_____

_____

_____

_____

_____

_____

_____

_____

_____

_____

_____

_____

_____

Day 63

"For if you forgive others their trespasses, your Heavenly Father will also forgive you. But if you do not forgive others then your Father will not forgive your trespasses."

Matthew 6:14

God of Forgiveness

Many of us have had things happen in our lives that has made it hard to forgive. Either being mistreated by a parent, spouse, friend or loved one. Abuse, rejection, or plain backstabbing. It hurts. And sometimes it's hard to get over it. My father and mother were divorced when I was four years old. He was never really in the picture after that. A Christmas kind of dad. I was in and out of hospitals a lot when I was young and not once did my father come to see me. When I got born again at 23 the first time, God impressed upon me to forgive him. "Forgive him? Why? What has he done for me?" Was what I was saying to God. You see the attitude in that statement? God want's you to forgive others, not for the person you are forgiving, but for you. (Matthew 6:14-15 When you forgive, truly forgive, you release the hurt that has been bottled up inside you. Do you have to accept that person into your life again? NO. But you do have to forgive.

Jesus died on the cross to forgive you of your sins. All of them. Yes, even those that nobody knows about. Those that you are ashamed of. All of them. He took stripes upon His back to the point that it had chunks of flesh removed so you could see bone; thorns pushed down onto His swollen, beaten face. Yes. Jesus came to die for us. He died a brutal death so we can be saved from our sins and live eternally in heaven. That's LOVE. You see, the word says, IF you forgive their trespasses (or sins) against you, then He will forgive yours, and you can be saved. BUT ONLY IF YOU FORGIVE FIRST.

God isn't trying to do anything but set you from the bondage of hurt, bitterness, pain, resentment. He wants to have you live a life of freedom and liberty. "Whom the Son sets free is free indeed." (John 8:36) Indeed means superabundantly. Peaceful. Wouldn't that be nice. Peace. The word of Jesus says, "My peace I leave with you. Not as the world gives peace" (John 14:27) Lay aside the hurt you have been carrying and ask the God of the universe to forgive anyone that you have ought against. He will heal your heart and draw you closer to Him. He is offering you everything that Jesus died to give you.

"Bear with each other and forgive one another if any of you has a grievance against someone. Forgive as the Lord forgave you."

Colossians 3:13

Write down those that you need to forgive and let it go.

_____

_____

_____

_____

_____

_____

_____

_____

_____

_____

_____

_____

_____

_____

_____

_____

_____

_____

Day 64

"And so we know and rely on the love God has for us. God is love. Whoever lives in love lives in god, and God in them."

1 John 4:16

Does God REALLY Love me and KNOW who I am?

A great question. Let's take a look at this. **Psalm 139:1-2** says, "O Lord, You have searched me and have known me. You know when I sit down and when I rise." **Jeremiah 12:3** says, "But You, O Lord, know me; You see me; and You examine the attitude of my heart toward You." You see! He knows your rising and your setting. He knows your heart and what the intent of it is. You cannot escape from God. He is always there.

Hebrews 4:13 says, "And no creature is hidden from His sight, but all are naked and exposed to the eyes of Him to whom we must give account." Account for what? YOUR LIFE! What you have done? What you have said? What you thought. What you didn't do. We ALL will give an account of our lives, whether good or bad. We will stand at the judgment seat of God. Now to some that's some scary stuff, but if you are a child of God, a believer in Jesus Christ His only begotten Son, and if you confess your sins and turn from them to start a new life in Christ Jesus, then the judgement seat isn't so scary because those who are forgiven and whose name is written in the Lamb's Book of Life will be saved from hell. And YES, hell is a very real place.

Unfortunately, many will be going there although it wasn't God's will for people to go there. The Bible says in **2Peter 3:9**, "The Lord does not delay and is not slow about His promise as some count slowness, but is patient towards you, not wishing for any to perish but for all to come to repentance." You see, God loves His creation so much that He was willing to send Jesus out of heaven to be born totally human, to live a life just like us, but with the sole purpose to die for all mankind. God doesn't want people to come to heaven and live out of fear; He came as a man to show how much He loves us. HE LOVES YOU. Yes. YOU just the way you are. You don't have to clean yourself up before He accepts you; He wants your brokenness. He wants your hurt. Your pain. He wants to heal you because He loves you.

John 3:16 says, "for God so loved the world that He GAVE His only begotten Son, that whosoever believe in Him shall have everlasting life." WOW!!! **Romans 10:9** says, "If you confess with your mouth that Jesus is Lord and believe in your heart that God raised Him from the dead, you will be saved."

Day 64

"Though the mountains be shaken and the hills be removed, yet my unfailing love for you will not be shaken nor My covenant of peace be removed." says the Lord, who has compassion on you."

Isaiah 54:10

Saved. Saved and on your way to heaven. What a glorious thought. Your sins are washed as white as snow and you can start a new. Even where you are you can start again. The bible says He loves you so much that He even numbers the hairs of your head. Can you imagine. That's love. So come just as you are, and let the LOVE of JESUS heal your soul.

Write down a love letter to God

_____

_____

_____

_____

_____

_____

_____

_____

_____

_____

_____

_____

_____

"Repent, then, and turn to God, so that your sins may be wiped out, that times of refreshing may come from the Lord."

Acts 3:19

Repent Repent

"Repent, repent," the cry goes out to the people from Jeremiah, Micah, Ezekiel, Isaiah, and new testament John the Baptist. "Repent, Repent" for destruction is sure to come to all those who choose not to believe and follow after God. It's as if God is saying through the entirety of the 66 books of the Bible.

Even in the days of Judges when everyone did what was right in their own eyes, (Judges 21:25) God loved them and sent Judges to help them. In the days of Isaiah and Jeremiah when the people were idol worshipers, He sent Nebuchadnezar to bring them to Babylon so they could know the bottom of the barrel (so to speak) and cry out to the only one who can bring them back again to serving Him.

"Repent, repent", God said in Chronicles, "If my people who are called by name, would humble themselves and turn from their wicked ways, I will hear from heaven and heal their land." (2 Chron 7:14) God only wants good for each of us. He wants a relationship of Love and Trust. That's why He calls us His bride. The most wonderful day in a couples life when they come together as one; in love with the expectancy of a life together sharing all their experiences and seeing the wonder of their lives unfolding together. Jesus is our groom and we are His bride. We are adorned with preciousness far greater than rubies. We will one day go to the wedding feast and present ourselves and feast at the Lord's table for eternity with our maker. He loves each one of us with a love that surpasses anything we as human can understand.

So take the time to look inwardly and examine yourself. Is there anything that you need to repent of? "Search me, O God, and know my heart; try me, and know my thoughts; And see if there be any wicked way in me, and lead me in the way everlasting," (Psalm 139:34-24)

"From that time on Jesus began to preach, "Repent, for the kingdom of heaven has come near,"

Matthew 4:17

What do you need to repent of?

_____

_____

_____

_____

_____

_____

_____

_____

_____

_____

_____

_____

_____

_____

_____

_____

_____

_____

_____

_____

"Master we worked hard all night and caught nothing but at Your word I will lower the nets. When they had done this, they caught a great number of fish and their nets were breaking."

Luke 5:5-6

Fishers of Men

Peter and the fishermen were out doing what they always do, catch fish. They were about their day in the usual way without thought of what the day would bring, but they weren't catching anything this day, and when your income is dependent on what you catch, the circumstances must have been frustrating. To be there all night and not catch anything, striving to make it happen. you can almost hear them saying, "Come on boys, lets wrap it up. Lets get the nets cleaned and go on home." BUT this was not going to be an ordinary night.

When coming close to shore, Jesus called from shore asking how their fishing went, and said to drop the nets on the right side of the boat. You could almost hear the collective sigh. They had just fished all night for nothing. They had just finished washing their nets, BUT Peter said, "Upon your word Lord, I will let down my net," (Luke 5:5) and the catch was so much that the nets were beginning to tare. Upon the encounter with Jesus, circumstances changed.

No matter what circumstances you are facing today, no matter how unsurmountable they may seem, when you inject Jesus into those circumstances, they will always change for the good. It's not immediate many times, but they do change. Slowly as you put your trust in God, and believe on the Lord Jesus Christ reading and studying His word for your life, then you will look back and see where Jesus led you through the situations and you will be able to see where He ordered your footsteps on the right path.

Peter and the fishermen didn't have any supply at the time, they didn't know what they were going to do, but Jesus is our abundant supplier in our times of need. The word says, "He will supply all your needs according to His riches in glory in Christ Jesus," Phil 4:19. If you are in need, turn to the Lord Jesus Christ who is our supply.

Day 66

"And whatever you ask in prayer, you will receive, if you have faith."
Matthew 21:22

What fish are you fishing for?

_____

_____

_____

_____

_____

_____

_____

_____

_____

_____

_____

_____

_____

_____

_____

_____

_____

_____

_____

_____

_____

"For I have chosen and sanctified (set apart for holy use) this house, and my eyes and my heart will be here perpetually." (2 Chron 7:16) Solomon had just finished the temple and it's dedication. God had a permanent house to dwell in. But God told Solomon, "If my people who are called by my name, shall HUMBLE themselves, PRAY, SEEK, CRAVE and REQUIRE AS NECESSARY My face, and TURN FROM THEIR WICKED WAYS, then will I hear from heaven, forgive their sin and heal their land. Now My eyes will be open and My ears attentive to prayer in this place."

They had a place to go and pray. They were able to go to a place where the presence of God was and have their petitions heard. We today have a so much better covenant with God. Upon the death, and resurrection of Jesus, we believers became the temple of God upon our confession of faith in Jesus. We are the temple set apart to holy use.

If we follow the commands to seek, pray, humble, and crave for His face; turn from wickedness, worldliness, and fleshliness, Jesus will hear from heaven, forgive our sins, and heal our land, our families, our bodies. Just as Jesus was speaking to Solomon, "Now my eyes will be open and My ears attentive to prayer in this place." We are the the ones now asking that our eyes be open and our ears to hear so we will know the direction in which He is calling us to .

What is that we all crave, but peace, love, and acceptance. We only find true love, true acceptance, and true peace in a true relationship with Jesus. Walking hand and hand with the author and developer of our faith. When we place our faith in Him, He has at that point set us apart to be holy. In holy living, we are then a light to those that are lost.

Set apart. Peculiar people. Holy. Righteous. That's who you are intended to be. And when you are, then all these things shall come upon you, for you are a child of the Most High God.

Day 67

God that mad the world and all things herein, seeing that he is Lord of heaven and earth, dwelleth not in temples made with hands:"

Acts 17:24

Write out a humble prayer to God.

_____

_____

_____

_____

_____

_____

_____

_____

_____

_____

_____

_____

_____

_____

_____

_____

_____

_____

"In all thy ways acknowledge Him, and He will direct your paths."

Proverbs 3:6

Paths of Righteousness

We have a state park near our home that has miles of hiking paths. It draws people from all over. Many of the trails are so well worn from the years of people traveling on them that they are smooth and level; an easy walk. But there are a few that are off the beaten path. These trails are the harder, deeper trails that are a little hidden. You have to go father distance to find them and work a little harder to walk them. They aren't an easy walk, the trails have a tendency to be overgrown and not as visible. You walk in amongst the brush and trees when all of a sudden the edge of the woods clears to a cliff edge that looks out over the valley below. The beauty of God's creation showing magnificently to all who have braved the harder path. The path that is less traveled, the path that is narrow.

In our Christian walk we are told that if we acknowledge Him, He will direct our paths. The word also says in Matthew 7:14, "But small is the gate and narrow the road that leads to life, and only a few find it." You see, the world offers so many distractions to a Christian's walk; music, television, sports, anything that takes the place of God and getting to know Him and His word more. It's a path of least resistance. It's a path of compromise, and a 'everyone else is doing it' mentality.

We as believers are to be set apart. Unique, a peculiar people. We are to travel the road less traveled. God didn't promise us a life of leisure, but a life where He guides us to a more fulfilling experience with Him. We are to travel the path that is not so well known, not the easiest, but when we come to the clearing on the cliff's edge and look out at the valley opened to our eyes, we can see clearly where God has led us.

God in His infinite mercy and love leads us where others will not travel to bring us to a deeper love, deeper relationship, and a deeper compassion for those that are lost. There are many who walk the road of least resistance, but it's in resistance that we become stronger, more in tune with our Father. Just like a diamond that is only created through compression and pressure, we become more like Christ when we take paths that are harder to travel and more difficult to see. Proverbs 20:24 says, "a man's steps are from the Lord; how then can man understand his way?" Psalm 17:5 says, "My steps have held fast to Your paths; my feet have not slipped."

"Keep steady my steps according to Your promise, and let no iniquity get dominion over me." Psalm 119:133

What paths have you taken that you can see the hand of God guiding you?

_____

_____

_____

_____

_____

_____

_____

_____

_____

_____

_____

_____

_____

_____

_____

_____

_____

_____

_____

_____

_____

_____

"I have told you all this so that ou may have peace in Me. Here on earth you will have many trails and sorrows. But take heart, because I have overcome the world."

John 16:33

Faith in God

As of this writing the world is going through a pandemic. Coronavirus is sweeping through countries, cities, and families. Many are sick and many more than we care to hear have died. It's a time of trials and sorrows. But, we must take heart because Jesus has overcome the world.

The word says in Jeremiah 30:17 "But I will restore you to health and heal your wounds, declares the Lord." In times of desperation we must trust that God is working all things together for good. My grandson attends a very small Christian school with only 38 children attending. The teachers and staff are God fearing men and women that love God and the kids. With the writing of this, the principle of the school passed away yesterday with Coronavirus. He fought hard for several weeks but was overcome. We have the assurance that He is with Jesus in heaven. Not an old man, not an overweight man, but a much loved man who left behind his personal and school family. Why? Because there is sin in the world. Why? Because we have fallible bodies. Why? Because sometimes even with our best efforts at prayer and belief, things don't go the way we want them to. That's when we have to trust God and believe by faith knowing that His ways are higher than our ways. His thoughts are higher than our thoughts.

2 Corinthians 5:7 says, "For we live by faith, not by sight." It's not the situations or circumstances that we go through that we live by. We have a hope and future in Christ, and in that hope we have eternal life. We are to look through what is happening to what our promises are in the Lord. Sometimes we don't understand what is happening but we are mandated by the Lord to trust that even in the hardest of situations He works ALL things together for good.

When your life seems out of control, turn to the only one that comforts, heals and walks with you. "Yea though I walk through the valley of the shadow of death, I will fear no evil; for Thou art with me; Thy rod and Thy staff they comfort me." The word promises in Deuteronomy 31:8 says, "The Lord himself goes before you and will be with you; He will never leave you nor forsake you. Do not be afraid; do not be discouraged,"

"So we say with confidence, "The Lord is my helper; I will not be afraid. What can mere mortals do to me?"

Hebrews 13:6

Are you walking by faith? In what way?

_____

_____

_____

_____

_____

_____

_____

_____

_____

_____

_____

_____

_____

_____

_____

_____

_____

_____

_____

"Put on God's whole armor that you may be able successfully to stand up against the strategies and the deceits of the devil."

Ephesians 6:11

What have you got on?

Hey there! Wait while I put my armor on for the day ok? (Ephesians 6:11) Got to put on my shoes. What's that? Why? Well because I'm preparing my feet with the gospel of peace. Ya, they help me on the path that I'm going. God directs my feet. What's that you asked? Oh, that's my belt of truth. I gird myself with it every day. You know Jesus is the truth. The word says if you know the truth, the truth will set you free. So that's why I make sure I have on the belt. What's this I'm putting on my chest? It's the breastplate of righteousness. This covers my heart and keeps it from the evil one. The truth says to guard your heart above all else. Why? Because out of it flows the issues of life. You say you like my hat? That's the helmet of salvation. I got this when I asked Jesus in my life. What's it do? It guards my thoughts. Satan tries to come at us through our thoughts so the helmet covers my mind so I can bring every thought into captivity. Then my thoughts will become agreeable with God's thoughts and my ways will be established and succeed. What's that in the corner? I don't go anywhere without that. It's my shield of faith. I use it daily to quench every thing that comes at me like arrows from Satan. No it doesn't bounce them off, it quenches them. Kind of like swallows them up like going into water. They get submerged and are useless. Satan sends all kinds of stuff my way but my shield protects me. Kind of cool huh! What? That? That's the most important part of my armor. That's the sword of the spirit. It's awesome. It's actually the word of God. As I wield it, I speak to situations and circumstances and they change. You see the Word of God, which is the sword of the spirit has power in the spoken word. Ya, like when God spoke the world into being. He spoke it and it happened. We speak truth, and then we act on the truth, and if we really believe what we are asking for, and it's in line with the word of God then we can have it. With the armor on, I am unstoppable because with God all things are possible. With it Satan can't touch me, and I go about doing good.

"He put on righteousness like a breastplate, and a helmet of salvation on His head; and He put on garments of vengeance for clothing and wrapped Himself with zeal as a mantle."

Isaiah 59:17

Ya, I wear it all the time. Who gave it to me? God did. When He gives us something we should definitely use it. You know, we fight the good fight every day with it. No not against each other, not against flesh and blood, but against principalities, powers, against rulers of wickedness in high places. We are supposed to be in the world but not of the world. What does that mean? Well, we aren't supposed to let this world and the things associated with the world influence us. We are supposed to influence them to be more like Christ and accept Jesus into their heart. You say you want one too? Awesome! All you have to do is say this, (Romans 10:9-10) Jesus I repent of my sin. I turn from my old way of doing things and I ask that you come into my heart and make my heart your home. I believe that you are the only begotten Son of God. I believe that you were born, died, and was raised after three days, and now because I believe in You I am born again. My name is written in the Lambs Book of Life. You said it? Praise Jesus. All of heaven is rejoicing with you right now. Wow!!! Look at that. There's your armor. Now you can put your armor on also. How about we put them on and go fight the good fight of faith and bring some good news to this lost and dying world.

So glad to have you added to the kingdom.

If you accepted Jesus as your savior, write a prayer of thanksgiving

---

Mahonia Plant

The plant on the front of the book is the Mahonia plant. As I was praying and asking God what He would have me to name my book, I drove into the driveway of my sister Linda's house. Right there in the middle of what looked like a wilderness, since it was the dead of winter, was a blooming bush. As I looked at this beautiful yellow plant blooming in the midst of lifeless, leafless trees, I saw Hope in the Wilderness.

When I looked up the qualities of the bush I was struck with the similarities to our Lord and Savior Jesus Christ. It is a useful barrier when planted as a hedge, much like the hedge of protection we get from our trust in Jesus from our enemies. It is also an ideal shelter for nesting birds which reminds me so much of Psalm 91

"He who dwells in the secret place of the Most High Shall abide under the shadow of the Almighty. I will say of the Lord, He is my refuge and my fortress; My God, in Him I will trust. Surely He shall deliver you from the snare of the fowler and from the perilous pestilence. He shall cover you with His feathers, and under His wings you shall take refuge; His truth shall be your shield and buckler."

I pray this book brings you hope in your time of wilderness.